Atomic Discipleship!

Prepare Your Church to Transform Neighborhoods and Nations

Scott Dalton, D.Min.

Atomic Discipleship! Prepare Your Church to Transform Neighborhoods and Nations

©2024 by Scott Dalton

Hikanos Press
113 Paramus Ave.
Newark, OH 43055

missioglobal.org

ISBN 13: 978-1-7361515-8-7
V. 1.0

All scriptures used, except where noted, are from The Holy Bible, New International Version®, NIV® Copyright © 2011 by Biblica, Inc.®.

Table of Contents

Introduction 4

1. "Mission Given, Mission Accomplished" 7

2. A Mature Disciple of Jesus 15

3. What Are You Aiming For? 23

4. Three Guiding Illustrations 33

5. Funnels and Cycles 41

6. Making Disciples—Mend the Nets! 51

7. Sending Capacity 65

8. Define, Design, Implement, Refine 73

9. The Entrance and the Exit 81

10. Making It Yours 89

Resources of Missio Global 97

Bibliography 101

Introduction

Writing this book has been a labor of love because I love Jesus and his body, the church. Jesus is the hope of the nations, but this hope is represented through his church throughout earth. The world sees Jesus through us. We are his ambassadors.

Jesus gave the church this mission by commanding us to "go and make disciples of the nations." He did not tell us to make converts, volunteers or even leaders—just go and make disciples of Christ. Making disciples, then, is the most basic element (and yet the greatest fulfillment) of the Great Commission.

Thinking about "atomic" discipleship may lead one to imagine explosive growth. And in the long-run this is true. But a definition of the word atomic in a dictionary typically begins with "very small, infinitesimal" because the atom is the smallest substance of any element. And yet the atom is the greatest source of power known on earth.

It is the same for discipleship. *The most basic element of the Great Commission is one disciple of Jesus sharing the gospel message with another person and then helping that new disciple grow in their walk with Jesus to the point that the newer disciple can do the same thing with yet another person.* Every Christian must be equipped to fulfill this mission. It is the commission of Christ to ALL of his followers. The Kingdom comes to earth one disciple at a time!

It is within the power and responsibility of church leaders to prepare their people for the work of ministry (Ephesians 4:12). The most basic element of ministry is being able to share the gospel, win someone to Christ, and then disciple that new follower of Jesus. Leaders are called to train their church members to do exactly this, which requires establishing a system to ensure this equipping takes place. We must not settle for anything less because this is THE mission that Jesus gave to his church.

Yet we see do not see this mission being fulfilled in most churches today. Every leader would say they are focused on making disciples, but is biblical discipleship happening in a systematic way in their church? How can we be preoccupied with so many other things in the "ministry" when this basic element of Jesus' mission for the church is still so lacking?

Leaders tend to focus on what they feel makes a "big" impact. There is nothing more explosive than atomic power. *But a long-term "big" impact requires "small" systematic discipleship.* There is no other option for long-term healthy spiritual growth that brings transformation.

The general level of spiritual maturity of church members in all nations lags where it should be largely because of a lack of effective discipleship. The negative impact of this lack of spiritual maturity is being clearly seen in our cultures. How will our churches empower disciples to reach people and be disciple makers? How will we prepare and send leaders? How can we plant many churches? The world needs us to do all these things!

This is not a missiology book or one that uncovers "secrets" of church growth from other places that we can import into the American church. Quite the opposite, this book looks at timeless and "placeless" biblical principles we must employ if we as the church are to be obedient to Jesus and the mandate he gave us until he returns. It's as simple as that. And the principles from Jesus are not complicated! But they are rarely seen in most churches. Could that be why it seems we are not making the impact we should be having?

This book *Atomic Discipleship* will have a companion book that is yet to be released entitled *Astounding Evidence*. *Atomic Discipleship* is the "method" book while *Astounding Evidence* will be the "message" book. *Astounding Evidence* will serve a vital purpose because we reproduce what we believe and who we are. However, it is best to start with a method book that you can apply to your present situation.

Our God and his Commission are still Great, and it's *for every church and every disciple of Christ in every nation.* It's what the world needs in this hour. The needs are great but the harvest is greater. Addition is long past being sufficient. We need multiplication. Let's get going!

Chapter 1

"Mission Given, Mission Accomplished!"

For a couple of the fourteen years my family lived in Brazil, we lived behind the residential complex of a Brazilian army base. Anytime I looked out our back windows I would read the bold motto of the army triumphantly painted in large clear letters on the wall of the base – *Mission Given, Mission Accomplished.* Their simple and clear mandate always led me to consider my own life. Do I have a clear sense of mission for my life? Am I accomplishing it during my days on earth?

God has marked out a path, a race, for each of his followers (Heb. 12:1) and has prepared specific works for each of us to accomplish during our journey on earth (Eph. 2:10). As we transition into the next phase of eternal life and stand before him, will we hear the precious words, "Well done, good and faithful servant! You accomplished the mission I gave to you!" That should be the life-long passion for every Christ-follower.

Just as God has prepared a mission for every person, Jesus has a mission for his corporate body, the church. Christ is the head and his body (the church) is made to follow his lead. And what is this mission? Some may say it's to follow the "Golden Rule" of treating others well as you would have them treat you, to be a "good person." Or more deeply, it could be expressed as loving God and loving others, the two Great Commandments as seen in the Old Testament and reiterated by Jesus. But these should be seen as guidelines for living, not a mission.

The mission of the church is clearly revealed in the final verses of the Gospel of Matthew, to "go and make disciples of the nations" (Matt. 28:19). This was the final command of Jesus to the apostles as recorded by Matthew. Other apostles would write other aspects of the commissioning of Jesus to his church, but the version by Matthew is the most known and also the most complete. It contains not just the command but also some basic steps on how to fulfill the it. It has become known as the Great Commission, and in truth it is the mission for every Christian congregation and disciple of Jesus across the face of the earth until Jesus returns.

Let's consider the gravity of what Jesus said in Matthew 28:18-19. After declaring "All authority in heaven and on earth has been given to me" he could have said anything! What do you think the apostles were expecting him to say? What would you expect him to say? Please catch the significance of what Jesus said. He said (in my words), "Because I have all authority now on earth, I'm giving you that same authority to go into all the nations and make disciples for me. This is the priority; it is your mission."

Jesus directly linked the Great Commission and spiritual authority. He gave us the mission and also the full authority to carry it out. Thinking conversely, the main reason he gives us delegated authority is to carry out the Great Commission to go and disciple the nations. The importance of this critical connection must be maintained front and center in our thinking about the purpose of the church and fulfilling its calling. (More on this topic in the forthcoming book *Astounding Evidence*.)

"Commission" Drift

Since the Great Commission call to go and disciple the nations is such a central part of the identity of the church, one would think that it would be well recognized by at least the majority of regular church attenders. However, a survey conducted in 2018 in the United States found that 51% of church attenders were not even familiar *with the expression* the "Great

Commission."[1] One in four respondents (25%) had heard of the term, but did not know to what it was referring. Only 17% knew the term and were familiar with the primary passage most recognized with the Great Commission as Matthew 28, "to go and make disciples of all nations."

I would not fault the average church attender for the results of this survey. The truth is they are not hearing or being taught about the commission of Jesus from the pulpit and they are rarely being equipped to take even the first steps in fulfilling it. Obviously, we have some work to do in preparing the church to recognize, embrace and actually fulfill the Lord's commission to every disciple of Jesus.

Action Steps for the Mission

The Great Commission as written in Matthew is unique in that it not only conveys the commission, but gives the basic steps on how to actually complete it. Taking a closer look at the text in Matthew 28:19-20 we find the verses contain four verbs—go, make, baptize, teach.

> Go therefore and make disciples of all nations, baptizing them in the name of the Father and of the Son and of the Holy Spirit, teaching them to observe (obey) all that I have commanded you. ESV (parenthesis added)

Let's start with the easy verbs. Baptizing and teaching are in the standard present participle form, a present action with the typical "-ing" ending in English. The verb "go" is not quite as clear. It also is a participle verb but is in a passive form. It reflects an action that has begun in the past but still continues. It also appears to be directly linked to the command of making

---

[1] https://www.barna.com/research/half-churchgoers-not-heard-great-commission/, accessed 02/02/2024.

disciples. The only command verb in this passage is "make disciples" as it is in the imperative form. Therefore, it will be customary in this text to keep "go" and "make" together in reference to the Great Commission. *Our goal is to make disciples who have the ability to go and make more disciples.*

Clearly the focus of the Great Commission is to make disciples. The other three verbs in this passage of Matthew could be used to describe the *actual process of making disciples*. The first step in making disciples is to go and find someone with whom to share the gospel message. We have to take the initiative. Second, the new convert should be baptized into the body of Christ and be welcomed into his new Christian family and community. Note that this is not a reference to becoming a member in a certain congregation or denomination. And third, the new believer needs to grow in their journey with Jesus through life-giving teaching based on believing and obeying the Word of God. This step is not just teaching them what Jesus said, but teaching them to *obey* what Jesus said. This is the life-long process of becoming more like Jesus and is at the core of fulfilling the command to make disciples. Making *converts* is NOT the command; we must make *disciples*.

There is one more important point about the verbs, and this is the real surprise. The word "make," the key verb in our passage, is not actually in the original language of Greek! The verb is directly "to disciple," meaning to teach or instruct someone. The Great Commission is to literally "disciple (teach) the nations" how to follow Jesus! Therefore, we could clarify Matthew 28:19-20 as follows:

> "Having gone (and continuing to go), disciple (teach) the nations (all people groups), baptizing them in the name of the Father and of the Son and of the Holy Spirit, teaching them to obey all that I have commanded you."

Combining the "Great Commissions"

Matthew is not the only apostle that recorded the command of Jesus to go and spread the gospel message. In fact, all fours authors of the Gospels (Matthew, Mark, Luke, John) included such a command and Luke even included a second one in Acts. Combining the "Great Commissions" provides valuable insight into how we are to fulfill the mission that Jesus has sent us on. The passages drawn from include Matthew 28:16-20, Mark 16:14-18, Luke 24:44-49, John 20:19-23, and Acts 1:8. Please study them on you own. They could appropriately be combined as follows:

> "In the power of the Holy Spirit (Acts), I am sending you (John) into all the world as my witnesses to proclaim the gospel (Acts/Mark), including repentance for the forgiveness of sins (Luke), and to make disciples of all nations (*ethnos*)[2], baptizing them and teaching them to observe all that I have commanded you (Matthew)."

Read this again slowly and reflect upon each thought. We need the power of the Holy Spirit to accomplish the mission! We must recognize that Jesus has sent us into the world just like the Father sent him. We must proclaim the good news, not be timid, going anywhere He sends us, sharing the message that forgiveness will be granted through the true repentance of sins. Our goal is to make disciples of Jesus (not us), integrating them into the blessed body of Christ in every nation. That is a mission worth living for, and even dying for.

Don't Neglect the Rest of Mark 16

While this combination of the Great Commission is certainly

---

[2] A race or nation forming a culture.

inspiring and constructive, as Great Commission workers we must not neglect the final few verses in Mark 16. Jesus declares beginning in Mark 16:17 that "these signs will accompany those who believe..." and then lists several acts that can only be completed through the supernatural power of the Holy Spirit, including casting out of demons and healing the sick. We must remember that the Gospel is not only a spoken message of repentance. It includes the miraculous power of God in action through us as disciples of Jesus. The cross of Jesus brought salvation, freedom and healing for the spirit, soul and body of everyone who receives him!

Some have framed this issue as a focus on the "Matthew 28" versus the "Mark 16" Great Commission. Whereas some churches or denominations tend to focus on the "teaching" aspect of discipleship, as represented in Matthew 28, other "streams" of the church tend to focus on "the signs" or supernatural aspects of the Gospel, as seen in Mark 16. The truth is we must have a balance of both. We need to create equipping opportunities that include solid, doctrinal training (which is highly critical in our time), but not at the expense of learning how to move and function in the supernatural. Conversely, we need to do more than only be "led by the Holy Spirit" when we disciple another person or get up to preach. We need to rightly manage the Word of God and learn how to perform practical ministry skills.

The Great Commission is the Mission of Every Church

The last 25 years or so has seen the tremendous rise of the "vision and mission" movement in the church. This movement was clearly "inspired" by the business world as every organization from small to large, for-profit to churches, have spent much time and effort on developing their mission, vision, and value statements. There is certainly some value in defining these declarations, and our organization, Missio

Global, has followed suit and done the same (more than once!). Such statements should give guidance to organizational leaders and clarity to employees and members.

At the same time, the mission statements of our churches should not vary too much because Christ already gave the mission for the church until His return—to go and make disciples of the nations. We must fully recognize that the Great Commission is not something just for the missions committee; it truly is the mission of every church, every day, until Jesus returns. All that we do should be screened through the lens of "how does this help us to go and make disciples?"

Every Church and Every Person

All disciples of Jesus have two basic callings in their lives: to be a minister of reconciliation and to make disciples. Every Christian is called to be an ambassador of God to the world and has given each of us "the ministry of reconciliation" (1 Cor. 5:18). We are also all clearly called to have a lifestyle of making disciples, as we have already seen. In the end, it is not even necessary to distinguish between the ministry of reconciliation (sharing the Gospel) and making disciples as they are both truly part of the same process.

The Great Commission is a *command*, not a suggestion, to every disciple of Christ. We are each called to be a disciple, which includes *making disciples who can make disciples*. Each of us has a unique style in the process because of the spiritual gifts we receive through the Holy Spirit. However, all believers must be intentional in making disciples. It's not just the responsibility of leaders. Church leadership is called to equip the saints to do the work of the ministry, and that ministry sits squarely on the call and ability of every disciple to make disciples.

Looking Ahead—Two Thoughts

Since the primary focus of the Great Commission is to go and make disciples, two primary thoughts come to mind. First, disciples must be *made*. Making disciples of Jesus must be intentional. And it takes time, so making disciples requires a process. The process of developing disciple makers is a main focus of this book.

Second, Jesus never spoke much about becoming a "leader." He didn't declare, "Go and make leaders of the nations." *Apparently it was enough for him to become his disciple!* You would never know that based upon the sheer volume of leadership material the church has been producing in the past couple decades (and I'm looking at myself as well). So it is worthwhile to take some time to examine what a true disciple of Jesus looks like since that is the desired outcome of the development process. To that we turn in the next chapter.

Chapter 2

A Mature Disciple of Jesus

In its simplest concept, to be a disciple is to be a student, to learn from a master. The Hebrew word for disciples (*talmidim*) has the meaning that the student doesn't just learn what their teacher *knows*, but becomes the type of person their teacher *is*.[3] As a Christian, our Master should only be the Lord Jesus. But being a disciple of Christ is much more than learning *about* Jesus; it is about learning *from* Jesus. It's true there is a valuable element of spiritual growth that we gain by learning from other disciples of Jesus, but that should never replace the personal relationship we have with Christ. Jesus longs for us to be with him. When he approached those whom he was calling to be his disciples, he used the simple, yet incredibly profound words of "follow me." He gives us the same call today.

We sometimes describe a true disciple of Jesus as a Christ-follower. We are to follow him and all his ways. We are to answer his call of "take my yoke upon you and *learn from me*, for I am gentle and humble in heart, and you will find rest for your souls" (Matt. 11:29). A yoke is a hard instrument of labor, but when we are yoked with Jesus our work with him is not a burden and we actually find rest! (For more discussion on being a disciple of Jesus, please see Lesson 1 in *CrossFire, A New Way of Living – Book 1* in the Missio Global discipleship series.)[4]

A true disciple will become like his teacher or master (Matt. 10:25). A disciple will do the same works as the master, and Jesus gave the promise to his disciples that they would do

---

[3] *Strong's Concordance*, word #8527.
[4] *CrossFire – Book 1*, Scott and Sherri Dalton (Hikanos Press, 2022).

even greater works (John 14:12). Clearly a major aspect of being like Jesus and doing his works is to be a disciple maker, not *to make* disciples, but *to be a maker* of disciples. A maker of disciple makers!

"There was a disciple at Damascus named Ananias"

A tremendous example of a mature disciple of Jesus can be seen in Acts 9 where we can learn from Ananias who lived in the city of Damascus. (This is not the Ananias of Acts 5!) In no biblical text is Ananias called a church leader. At that time in Damascus the fellowship of believers was still in its early stages, and the role of Ananias is never specified. He is simply called "a disciple" (Acts 9:10). Ananias was chosen by Jesus to be the first disciple to meet with Saul (who later becomes Paul) after Saul's encounter with Jesus on the road to Damascus. Up to that time, Saul was a well-known violent persecutor of the followers of Jesus and was heading to Damascus for that very purpose. Let's examine some important characteristics of a disciple of Jesus as seen in the life of Ananias.

A Disciple Understands and Obeys the Logos[5] Word of God

Let's begin by looking at Paul's own testimony in Acts 22 of the events that took place in Acts 9. Paul described Ananias as "a devout man according to the law, well-spoken of by all the Jews" (Acts 22:12). In this testimony of his conversion, Paul was clearly contextualizing his testimony to a Jewish audience (he was being arrested in Jerusalem). But it can be concluded that Ananias knew well the written word of God, which Paul would describe as the Law. This is the *logos* word

---

[5] *Strong's Concordance*, word #3056.

of God. A mature disciple of Jesus studies and knows well the Bible, the written Word of God.

A Disciple Has a Positive Reputation in the Church and Community

Also from this passage in Acts 22, it is safe to conclude that Ananias was held in good regard among the fellowship of believers in Damascus and likely in the community at large as he was "well-spoken of by all the Jews" (Acts 22:12). A mature disciple does their best to maintain a good reputation, as far as they can control.

A Disciple Can Discern the Voice of the Lord (the Rhema[6] Word of God)

Perhaps the most striking aspect of this account of Ananias is how clearly he discerns the voice of the Lord. The text describes Ananias' leading from Jesus as coming in a "vision," which clearly was not a dream in this case. Based on the minimal biblical accounts we have of Ananias, we don't know if this was a frequent experience for Ananias or not. However, from this text in Acts 9, it does not seem he reacted to Jesus speaking so directly to him as an unusual occurrence. Ananias quickly and clearly recognized the voice of the Lord calling to him. This ability only comes when a Christ-follower is accustomed to speaking to and hearing from the Lord. A mature disciple learns how to confidently discern the voice of the Lord from all the other voices they are hearing.

A Disciple Has a "Friend" Relationship with the Lord

This characteristic of Ananias is related to more than his ability to discern God's voice. It has to do with the degree of

---

[6] *Strong's Concordance*, word #4487.

relationship he has with the Lord. Evangelist Mark Swiger calls this a "friend relationship."[7] As recorded by Luke in Acts, the Lord called Ananias simply by his first name, and Ananias responds very calmly. When he is unsure of the Lord's request, he simply asks a question of the Lord. It is a conversation, clearly between a master and a servant, but in a rather friendly tone. A mature disciple is able to simply go for a walk and converse with Jesus.

A Disciple Obeys the Leading of God Even When It Doesn't Seem to Make Sense

We know in our minds that God sees more than we do, but so many times it's hard for our hearts to really believe it! It is a matter of trust; do we really trust God in every situation? Trust is another way to describe faith. Faith and fear can never coexist. If you are in fear you cannot be in faith. Ananias was concerned because he had heard of the dangerous Saul. So he asked God just to be sure! And the Lord told Ananias that basically he was an answer to prayer (see Acts 9:11-12). A mature disciple understands that he can be an answer to someone's prayer every day and let the Holy Spirit lead him, even when it seems like a risk or seems dangerous.

A Disciple Knows How to Minister in the Supernatural

Ananias obeyed and went to track down the house where Saul was staying. When he found Saul, Ananias confidently laid his hands on Saul, made a faith-filled declaration, and two things happened: Saul received his sight again and he was filled with the Holy Spirit. Ananias clearly was confident in ministering in the supernatural. This example shows a healing

---

[7] *What is a Disciple and How Do You Make One?*, Mark Swiger (Lake Mary, FL: Creation House, 2015), 12. This book provides a thorough analysis of the qualities of a disciple of Jesus.

(in a sense a spiritual healing also) and what could be described as the baptism in the Holy Spirit. Although not clearly indicated in the text, from the greater context of the book of Acts, this account likely indicates that Saul began speaking in tongues through this encounter with Ananias. A mature disciple can confidently minister in the supernatural.

A Disciple Knows How to Administer Water Baptism (Practical Ministry)

It is clearly seen in this account that Ananias baptized Saul immediately after this prayer encounter with Saul. "He rose and was baptized" (Acts 9:18); "And now why do you wait? Rise and be baptized and wash away your sins, calling on his name" (Acts 22:16). Ananias understood the directives of Jesus and the Apostles and promptly obeyed by leading Saul into water baptism. Again, we do not know the role of Ananias in the fellowship of believers in Damascus, but the "church" was likely still very organic (not structured). In today's church, administering water baptism is typically reserved just for pastors. However, a mature disciple should understand the spiritual dimensions of water baptism, be able to explain it doctrinally, and be confident to water baptize a new believer when the necessity or opportunity arises.

A Disciple Can Operate in the Prophetic

Scripture never calls Ananias a prophet, but he certainly operated in the prophetic. The Lord directed Ananias to speak a word from Him to Saul. Ananias clearly received the word and confidently delivered it to Saul. He gave a truly strong prophetic word that gave Saul a clear calling from the Lord and direction for his life. Operating in the prophetic is a spiritual gift of the Holy Spirit that is available to every disciple. This is not that same as being a prophet according to Ephesians 4:11, but because the Holy Spirit resides in us, every disciple has the capacity to hear from the Holy Spirit and bring a word of encouragement or confirmation to another person. This should generally ***not*** be a word of correction (see 1 Cor. 14:3). A mature disciple will be ready to hear from the Lord and act in this manner.

A Disciple is Committed to Reach Their Community

Saul stayed in Damascus for "some days" (Acts 9:19b) and immediately began to preach Jesus as the Son of God in the synagogues. It certainly created an uproar among the Jewish community in the city! Although not specifically cited in the text, Saul most likely stayed in the home of Ananias during this period. This was obviously a risk to Ananias (and his family if present). Even if Saul didn't stay in the home of Ananias, it was still a risk for Ananias and all the other disciples in Damascus. After "many days had past" (Acts 9:23), the Jews plotted to kill Saul, but he escaped the city with the help of the disciples.

The church is often praying for revival as if that will be the answer to all the problems in the world. The truth is that revival (or awakening) more often than not brings risk and persecution to believers. A mature disciple stands firm in faith to express the love of God to their community, even at the risk to their reputation, breaking of relationships, and physical risk.

A Summary of a Mature Disciple of Jesus

The above nine characteristics of Ananias in Acts 9 could be simplified into these categories. A mature disciple of Jesus:

- Has a vibrant and life-giving *relationship with Jesus*. He has learned to discern the voice of Jesus and looks forward to being with Jesus.

- Studies and knows the *Bible*, remembering that he is not just studying a document, but is wanting to better know Jesus, who is the Word.
- *Obeys* the direction of Jesus as his Lord, even when it doesn't make sense, is a risk, or is even dangerous. His motivation is love for Jesus and love for people!
- Maintains a positive *reputation* (inside and outside of the church) and seeks to serve and reach his community for Christ.
- Is able to function in the *supernatural*, such as in healing and the prophetic. He has learned his predominant spiritual gifts and has grown in experience in operating in them.
- Has been trained in the *practical ministry* of the church. He is able to administer ministries such as water baptism, leading small groups, and preparing a basic preaching.

These should be the type of characteristics that we're attempting to develop in the members of our churches. These characteristics are not easy to measure, but it is possible! And it is vital if our aim is to complete the mission Jesus gave us of making disciples of the nations.

Satisfied with "Good and Faithful" Church Attendees

Unfortunately, too many church leaders are comfortable with "good and faithful" church members rather than true mature disciples. We sometimes hear about discipleship and the importance of sharing our Christian faith, but evangelism is reduced to inviting someone to church and discipleship becomes a ten-week class in a church room (at best). We are told that God has created us for a purposeful life, but rarely is an avenue given to discover, develop, and employ this purpose.

Dr. J. Lee Simmons, a church-planting pastor for over 30 years and founder of Missio Global, tells of the time when God challenged him by asking, "You're satisfied with someone being a faithful church member, aren't you?" Pondering the question, Simmons responded, "Well, I guess I am," to which God firmly said, "I'm not!" Let us heed this word.

If attendance is at least steady, finances are stable, and people are serving once a month, we are pleased or at least not stressed. Seems like smooth sailing for now at least. We need to not be satisfied with *anything less* than a focus on doing *everything possible* to make disciples of *every person* in the church, equipping them to go and make disciples.

Now that we have a clear understanding of the mission of the church—to go and make disciples—and what a mature disciple looks like, we must ask two hard questions of ourselves: "Is that indeed the goal in my church? And are we succeeding?" Take a deep breath and let's proceed.

Chapter 3

What Are You Aiming For?

No one ever enjoys an evaluation. Whether it be a job review, a medical exam, or even unsolicited "feedback" from your spouse! But review and evaluation is an essential part of health and growth in all aspects of life. All healthy life grows and reproduces. We should expect this of ourselves, our churches and our ministries.

Looking for Signs

There's a long list of common church "vital signs," including weekly attendance in the services, number of visitors, number of salvations, number of water baptisms, new members, participation in small groups, number of people serving in a ministry, income, etc. Churches often track these basic measures just like a physician will check and track the vital signs of her patient. They are valid indicators of general church health. As has been said, "Numbers don't mean everything, but they do tell a story."

However, these measures do not directly measure the church's success in fulfilling the Great Commission of going and making disciples. They reveal trends of growth or decline, but provide no prescriptive reasons for the growth or decline. They measure effects, but provide no indication of the causes. Why is attendance down (or up)? Why did we only have 20 people baptized last year (or this might be good for a brand new church)? *And most dangerous of all, we could be feeling really good about the positive signs in our measures, but still*

NOT be fulfilling our mission of going and making disciples because our measures are not based on that clear goal.

The Crisis of the "80% Hole" for New Believers

The ultimate case in point of not having all the right measures in place is the fact that our churches are losing 80% of new coverts within 90 days of their decision for Christ. You read that correctly. The truth is that all empirical and anecdotal data shows that *at least* 80% of new converts are walking away from faithfulness to God and church attendance within 90 days of their salvation decision.[8] This is the case in churches across the world—denominational, cultural, degree of economic or educational levels, or any other locational factors do not make a difference.

Imagine Simon Peter and Andrew in the story of the great catch of fish in Luke 5 seeing this astonishing catch of fish in their nets only to lose over 80% of them as they pull their nets into their boats. That's the reality in our churches today. *We have an 80% hole in our nets*, which is truly a crisis. Of every *five* people who raise their hand or respond in some way to a call for salvation in your church, on average only *one* of them is standing firm in their faith 90 days later.

Rest assured this issue will be addressed fully later in Chapter 6 about discipleship, but for now let's continue the discussion on measurements.

Values → Goals → Measures

The truth is that every church leader must grapple with the question, "What does success look like in my church?" The

---

[8] *Discipleship That Works*, Grant Edwards (Springfield, OH: Specificity Publications, 2024), 11-16.

answer reveals your goal, and you hit what you're aiming at. Nearly every church leader would say their goal is to make disciples, but that is typically not reflected in what is being measured in most churches today. The typical key measures track simple numeric participation in various levels of engagement of church participants (the assimilation funnel which is examined in Chapter 5). It is true that these measures are the easiest to track, but in the end it reveals that our measures are based on simple quantitative goals.

And those goals reveal the values of the church, what is truly important to the church leadership. If a church is only tracking the basic numeric statistics as mentioned above, then that's what it will get—growth (or decline) in participation of the various activities. But this only demonstrates the church's ability to draw a crowd and maintain participation. It reveals very little about the true spiritual health of the church (not to mention its members) or its success in completing the Great Commission.

What you are aiming for determines what you measure. According to the commission given by Jesus, we should be aiming to make disciples who have the ability to go and make more disciples. The hard truth is that most churches need to adjust their "scorecard" of what they are measuring if they truly want to obey the Great Commission. However, the correct goals must first be established. Then the church can set measures that align with the Great Commission goals and promote to the congregation the actions that correspond with the new measures. All this must be based on prioritizing the value of obeying *in a practical way* the Great Commission of going and making disciples.

The Goal of a True Great Commission Church

Jesus told the disciples that he had made to go and make more disciples. This is the clear mandate to the Church (the worldwide body of Christ). But we must not misapply this mandate as being directed strictly to the organization of the local church. As we have seen, the commission is to each individual believer. All disciples of Christ are to be his ambassadors, as if God is making his appeal through each one of us (because he is). In other words, the Great Commission is *disciples* going and making disciples; it is not *churches* making disciples. *The goal of a true Great Commission church should be to equip and support disciples to go and make disciples (locally and globally).* Anything less will never surpass addition, whereas God's call and the world's need demands multiplication.

Yes, the local church will still organize corporate activities and events including weekly worship and celebration times, equipping opportunities, and outreaches. But the capacity of the church to be obedient to its call to go and make disciples will be extremely constrained if those activities are the *primary* drivers of numerical "growth" in the church. True and healthy growth should be driven *largely* by the disciples in the church (which should be the vast majority of the members) who are capable to go to those around them in everyday life, effectively share the gospel, and nurture new believers to maturity in Christ.

As the use of the words "primary" and "largely" in the previous paragraph indicate, this is not an either/or issue. A local church will use all their resources and points of contact to reach their community, bring people to Christ, and provide opportunities for spiritual growth. But the key is to maintain focus *on the mission*—to go and make disciples who can go and make disciples. Church "growth" that does not achieve this mission is not the healthy and mature growth that Jesus seeks. What you measure will determine what kind of growth you will have—simply numeric in participation, or the effective "equipping of the saints (disciples) for the works of ministry" Eph. 4:11-13).

What You Measure and Celebrate Will Drive Your Growth

The bottom line is that what a church measures is what will receive attention. This, in turn, is what is likely to generate numerical growth (or decline). So as we have discussed, the goals that you are aiming for and the related measures are critical decisions that determine the type of growth or decline a church will experience.

But less obvious is another truth in church growth—what you *celebrate* is a powerful contributor to growth. In fact, likely even more so than what is measured because of the emotional rewards that come with celebration. Think of all the reasons that someone may be called to the front of a church service for celebration and recognition. It could be new members, those who were baptized, people who completed a class or training. It could even be people who participated in a special retreat or conference. Is volunteerism highly celebrated in the church? Or leading small groups? Few experiences will give the emotional reward that comes from celebration and recognition. The church greatly influences the actions of the members by celebrating what it deems as important behavior.

With this in mind, take a moment to consider what is celebrated in your church. Is there *anything at all* that is connected to making disciples who are capable of making other disciples outside of a classroom setting? As examples, is there any mechanism that recognizes the number of people reached for Christ through personal evangelism, or new believers growing through personal discipleship? Are there disciples who have completed an equipping opportunity (like evangelism training) in the church that raises the ministry skills of members in the church? Does the church have a focused outreach to extend the impact of the church and are the ministry workers celebrated? *What is celebrated will receive the attention of the church members and drive church growth*. Leadership must make sure that what is celebrated is achieving the mission that Christ has given the church of going and making disciples.

Micro Goals and Macro Goals

Todd Wilson and Dave Ferguson present an in-depth analysis of goals and measures in their book *Becoming a Level Five Multiplying Church Field Guide*.[9] Wilson and Ferguson break down healthy church growth (which they call Kingdom growth) into micro and macro elements. In general, the micro level addresses the actions of individual people in the local church while the macro level involves church-wide, structural actions. Further, both the micro and macro levels include elements of addition and multiplication. A simple description brings clarification.

Micro-addition is simply a disciple who personally wins a non-Christian to Christ. This disciple understands the full Gospel message and is able and comfortable to share it with someone who is not following Christ. This is addition to the Kingdom, and hopefully the church, at the micro (individual) level. Micro-addition is the bedrock, the foundation of basic Christianity. It is the fulfillment of the call to go and make disciples.

Micro-multiplication enters when the new Christ-follower is prepared to do the same with another person who is not currently following Christ. There does not necessarily need to be a long time gap before this person is able to at least somewhat effectively share Jesus with another person. The new "soul-winner" continues to walk in relationship with the person who is discipling him as he begins to disciple the newer

---

[9] *Becoming a Level Five Multiplying Church Field Guide,* Todd Wilson, Dave Ferguson, with Alan Hirsch (Franklin, TN: Exponential.org, 2015), see chapter 2.

Christ-follower (or they can meet as a micro-group for discipleship). The net result is that *multiplication has begun* at the micro level, and we have the seedbed for multiplication at the macro level. *Micro-multiplication must be a critical goal for every church which seeks to fulfill the mission of the Great Commission.* It should be a, if not *the*, primary driver of church growth.

Macro-addition is about building capacity within the local church for making biblical disciples. Examples include training where *disciples are equipped* to share their faith and make disciples. This training is NOT to do the discipling, but to train disciples to make disciples, although this skill is largely gained through actual personal discipleship. A clear process for training emerging leaders is another element. The goals, measures, and what's celebrated by the church that support making disciples are included in this category, as well as the church budget.

And finally, macro-multiplication is about adding capacity for making biblical disciples beyond the existing local church. This represents the "macro" sending capacity of the church. This is where the church moves beyond an adding-accumulation focus to a releasing-sending focus.[10] It is where the church enters into reproduction and potentially into multiplication. *Less than 5% of churches ever achieve this stage*, but it should be a goal for every healthy church.[11]

These four areas for goals are not a continuum; they should be happening simultaneously. However, they are sequential. You can't arrive at healthy macro-addition or multiplication without micro-addition and multiplication, where disciples are *actually making disciples*. So a wise church leadership will seek to *set goals* that can be *measured by actions* (or indicators) in each of these four areas.

---

[10] *Becoming a Level Five Multiplying Church Field Guide,* 61.
[11] *Becoming a Level Five Multiplying Church Field Guide,* 29-30.

What are some goals and measures that a church focused on the Great Commission (going and making disciples) could set for itself? At the micro level, reconsider the characteristics of a mature disciple examined in Chapter 2. A disciple should be growing in their knowledge of the Bible, able to share the Gospel, be personally investing in another growing disciple, growing in their spiritual gifts, and reaching out to their community. Below is an example of a goal and measures of success for micro-addition.

Goal for Micro-Addition:
- o Church members are faithful disciples who can win and disciple another person.

Measurements for Micro-Addition
(*actions that indicate* the church is meeting this goal):
- o 90% of members are regularly praying for at least one person not following Jesus.
- o 80% of members are regularly reading their Bible (at least 5 days per week).
- o 70% of members have completed an 8 to 12-week foundational discipleship study in *a one-on-one or micro-group setting* and are capable of leading someone else through the study.
- o 70% of members clearly understand the Gospel and are able to effectively share it with others.
- o 60% of members participate in a small group that facilitates and supports discipleship relationships.
- o 50% of members will share the Gospel with at least one person or pray with a person not following Christ for a need they have every quarter (every three months).

As you can see, these are not typical measures of church success, but they do a much better job of measuring if the church is achieving its mission of going and making disciples. I guarantee that if the church is even getting close to achieving these goals, it will be a growing church!

One additional point is important. The church should make sure that good biblical doctrine is taught in the church and is being passed on in the small groups and discipleship relationships. The church in general is in a crisis of a lack of a biblical worldview. We must radically stand firm on godly, biblical principles and truth.

We will not take the time here to provide examples of goals and measures in the other three areas, but you can do that on your own with your leadership team. We have one more chapter before we get into the "nuts and bolts" of developing a process for discipleship and leadership development.

Atomic Discipleship

Chapter 4

Three Guiding Illustrations

Before we launch into the practical steps of developing a system for making disciples who have the ability to go and make disciples, let's look at a few "guiding illustrations." I believe you will come to see that these will serve as lamps along the path of this journey.

Wine and Wineskins

The purpose of a parable is to illustrate one major point, and, as such, should not be interpreted allegorically with every detail representing something else. The primary point to take away from the parable of the wine and the wineskins is that something new (the spiritual life that comes from the new birth of the New Covenant) was not going to fit well within the structure of the old religious mindset and practices. From this perspective, we can say that the wine represents vibrant, true spiritual life a person experiences through Jesus, and the wineskin represents the religious structures in which the Christ-follower lives out their spiritual life.

The simple purpose of a wineskin is to contain wine. The spiritual vitality of the "wine" (life in Jesus) needs a structure to hold it. In fact, without an appropriate structure to hold it, the wine is spilled on the ground and wasted. Jesus is clearly concerned in this parable that both the wine and the wineskins be preserved (Mt. 9:17). However, it is clear the most important of the two is the wine. Without the wine, a wineskin is at best a nice piece of craftsmanship, but has little practical value.

On a personal level, this structure may include spiritual disciplines such as Bible reading, prayer, and the choices a person makes to live in holiness. A true disciple of Christ will endeavor to establish fruitful habits in their spiritual life. But in all cases, the ultimate goal of this structure is to contain the growing life they have in Jesus. The potential danger of focusing too rigidly on these spiritual disciplines is like esteeming the wineskin as more important than the wine. That is a trap that leads to legalism and a religious, judgmental spirit.

The concept of the wine (life in Jesus) and the wineskin (spiritual structure) can, of course, be applied at the local church level, which is our primary focus in this discussion. It is certainly the goal of every godly church leader that church members, and even guests, experience the abundant life that Jesus declares is ours in Him. At the great risk of being misinterpreted, we want the "wine" to flow freely! We want people to experience the presence of God and see many lives healed and transformed through the power of Holy Spirit. Without a doubt, the wine IS the most important thing, but without some structure it is wasted on the ground, meaning the lasting impact is not conserved. How many times have we seen little lasting impact of a move of God?

The church tends to error in the extremes. I have seen numerous churches in different moves of the Holy Spirit swing so hard to the side of the "wine" that pretty much any structure goes out the window. While that certainly may be the desire of God for a time because He wants to remind us that He actually wants to lead our times together, Jesus was clear that the wineskin (structure) is essential to maintain the wine. The danger occurs when a leader begins to think that all their church growth problems will be solved simply when "the Lord shows up" in the services. Too often that ends up becoming a situation where the leader ends up trying to manipulate the church members.

But clearly the opposite is true as well. In fact, much of church history shows that we have tended to focus much more on the "wineskin" of church structure, to the point that in certain eras it didn't seem to matter to the "church" if there was any wine left at all! I suppose it could be said that we can control that part more than we can control the wine so it receives more of our attention. But an excessive focus on church structure (the wineskin) without maintaining in the center of our understanding the purpose of the structure (to hold the wine) only leads to empty religious practices and rituals, and eventually an empty wineskin.

An important aspect of the wineskin (structure) is that it determines our capacity to receive more wine, which I would describe as the church's capacity to make and send disciples. When we are faithful in making disciples and building our sending capacity, I believe God will send us more. Could it be that God withholds an "outpouring" of Holy Spirit because the wineskins of our churches could not hold it?

Structure is more than important; it is *necessary* to hold the wine. *But we don't consume the wineskin!* And yet, how much time and effort do churches put into creating and improving a beautiful, shiny wineskin? Investing time and money into developing the wineskin is absolutely valid, but not at the expense of neglecting the wine. The purpose of the wineskin (structure) is to lead people into consistent, heart transforming spiritual growth. If that is not happening, the church attendees may remain satisfied for a time in their infatuation of a beautiful, consumer-driven wineskin. But disciples are not being made, and the church is failing in its mission.

The Parable of the Sower

One of the best known parables of Jesus, the parable of the sower is so rich and deep there is certainly much to dig into. Generally a parable about the Kingdom of God, Jesus spoke about four types of people, represented by four types of soil, and how the Word of God impacted their lives. As such, the parable seems to be about evangelism. But further examination shows that it seems more about the process of discipleship.

As the wineskin from the previous parable reveals characteristics of church *structure*, the four soils of this parable reveal important stages in the *process* of becoming a disciple of Jesus. A process is dynamic and in motion. Picture in your mind a person passing through the stages of the four soils in this parable.

The first soil is the hard path. This is the path well-traveled by those who are not seeking the things of God. This is the broad path that leads to destruction (Mt. 7:13) and those who travel along it seem to be set in an unbiblical worldview. The ground is hard; the seed of the Word does not easily enter. The is no spiritual conversion, no salvation, with this soil in the parable. The main thing to gain from this soil is that the devil always has a follow-up plan. So our follow-up plan needs to be better than his!

The second soil is the rocky ground. The soil is shallow, but it's enough for a seed to germinate and sprout up. In fact, the word is received with joy and new life sprouts up quickly despite at least some of the rocks being below the ground level (where other people cannot see them). I believe this soil reveals the greatest warning to us in the parable.

It is clear that a spiritual conversion takes place with this second soil; this person becomes saved. It isn't just that they received well the word and were open to it. There is a clear salvation experience here. They had obvious difficulties in their life (the "rocks" of life) and received the Gospel with joy, seeing it as the answer to their problems. The seed sprouted, there was new life, but they were "scorched" and "fell away" because their roots could not pass through the rocks in their life to reach the stream of life. Everyone will encounter difficulties and persecution. So our spiritual roots (which are unseen) must be able to reach the stream of God's sustaining water. Luke says in 8:13, "they believe for a while, and in time of testing fall away." This is not a theology class, but Jesus sounds pretty clear about what happened. Our main lesson from this soil is that people are going to need help getting the rocky places out of their lives after salvation. If not, no matter with what joy they received the word, their salvation is at risk of not being maintained.

Unfortunately, the third soil describes the type of people that are frequently in our churches. The third seed has survived the "birds" in the hard path and the scorching sun of persecution and trials. They have more than sprouted; they have now grown and become a tall plant or crop. They certainly give to the church, perhaps even tithe, and are probably consistently serving as well. But it is likely they rarely open the Bible at home and spend personal time with God, with the result being the things of God are not their passion. They have not removed the worldly weeds as they have grown in their spiritual life, seeing them as no big deal, as "they go on their way" (Lk 8:14). They have become choked, unfruitful, not useful for the Kingdom. They have allowed themselves to become ensnared by the cares of the world, the deceitfulness of riches, and pleasures of life. "Their fruit does not mature" (Lk 8:14).

The challenge for the church in regard to these "third soil" believers is that we may have built them into our structures and depend on them for the success of church activities. First of all, we need them for our attendance statistics. We also need them to volunteer to serve in church ministries, especially during the services. And of course, we need their financial giving. They generally don't cause problems, so as long as they stay happy with the church programs and stay involved, we don't really expect anything more from them. But God does, and it's the responsibility of the church to challenge them and provide a growth path. The main lesson we can take from this soil is that the church must provide a vehicle for spiritual accountability for people at this level (challenge them to cut down the weeds!) and a pathway for taking new steps in their faith and assuming greater responsibilities in ministry.

The fourth soil is what we all strive for, first in our personal lives and then in the church. Amen for the hundredfold! That may sound a bit frivolous, but it's critical to remember that Jesus is radical about each of us bearing spiritual fruit. This soil "produced grain" and that's what Jesus expects of His disciples. He said that bearing *much fruit* is the proof of being His disciple (Jn. 15:8). The unfruitful branch He takes away and even the fruitful branch He will prune (Jn. 15:2). This is the lesson we need to take from this soil. We must hold high the standard that God expects His disciples to bear eternal fruit, and we must provide a clear avenue for our people to achieve it.

It's valuable to examine the characteristics detailed in the parables about this soil. This person "hears the word and understands it" (Mt. 13:23), hears the word and accepts it (Mk. 4:20), holds it (the word) "in an honest and good heart" (Lk 8:15). Clearly, the first step is hearing, receiving and understanding the Word. But that is not the end. The person "bears fruit and yields" (Mt. 13:23). More than simply learning the Word, they have been equipped to act! People do not simply need teaching; they need *training*. And Luke adds bearing fruit "with patience" (Lk. 8:15). We need patience because it's a process. But the Lord of the harvest is good and faithful to equip us as we seek Him diligently.

Lower Room versus Upper Room

Well known church consultant Will Mancini has developed a very helpful illustration that clarifies the different elements of typical church life. Mancini identifies what he considers the four most common reasons people connect with a church:

place, personality, programs and people.[12] Place relates to the convenience of the church's location. Personality typically has to do with how the attendee connects with or admires the church leader. Programs is an obvious reason, often related to the kid's or youth ministry of the church. People has to do with friends or family that may also attend the church.

These are the common reasons people enter the "front door" of a church and cause them to connect to the church. While these are all important and valid aspects of church life, in and of themselves these reasons will not keep a person committed to the church in the long-term because any of the aspects *can change*. People move to the other side of town, pastors retire or leave, kids grow up and friends change or move.

People who stay in a church *only* for one or more of these four reasons may be happy with their church, but it is highly unlikely they will be truly passionate about their church. Why? Because they never moved into Mancini's fifth reason for staying in a church—purpose. Purpose goes far beyond the front door into a deeper reason to remain committed to a church (or movement) for many years.

Mancini describes the four common reason as taking place in the "Lower Room" of the church while purpose takes place in the "Upper Room." Both "rooms" are important. These are the "ports of entry," if you will, that lead people to be interested in attending and staying in a church. An accessible location is helpful, the pastor should be caring and able to teach, good programs are important, and the congregants should be friendly. But church leaders should not be content to allow people to remain a long time in the lower room because people will never reach their personal purpose and calling in life by staying in the lower room. Therefore, the church must create and clearly communicate a "staircase" by

---

[12] *Future Church*, Will Mancini and Cory Hartman (Grand Rapids: Baker Books, 2020), 22.

which a person can ascend from a "lower room" reason for being in the church to begin living in the "upper room" purpose.

The goal of the church should always be to move people into the *eternity-focused* upper room. This is where transformation takes place; where self-centered values become exchanged for eternal values. And what is the purpose of a church? Mancini calls it "God's unique disciple-making vision for a church."[13] Remember, the mission of every church is the Great Commission of making disciples. But each church will express and live the Great Commission in a unique way that God has established for it. When church members begin to live in this upper room vision, they move beyond the temporary reasons of place, personality, programs and people. They will stay, or be sent out, with a passion because they are fulfilling their calling in God through the church ministry!

---

[13] *Future Church*, 29.

Chapter 5

Funnels and Cycles

In the past 40 years, evangelical churches in the West have developed an amazingly uniform organizational structure. And whether for good and bad, much of the rest of the Christian church around the world still looks to the West as the primary example of how church should function. Not coincidentally this homogenizing of structure and process has occurred in unison with the rise of the mega-churches. Thousands of people passing through the doors of the church building every week requires a new way of organizing them.

Arguably more than any other source, the release in 1995 of *The Purpose Driven Church* by Rick Warren seemed to cement in place the current pattern of church. Warren's pattern has five concentric circles, from community to core, representing increasing levels of engagement that people have with a church. In 2006, *Simple Church*, by Thom Rainer and Eric Geiger, streamlined the general pattern into three levels. And this three-stage (some have made it four-stage) "assimilation funnel" remains the standard today, to the point that it's hard to envision church in a different structure, at least for Christians in the West.

Based on the concept of a sales funnel, the broadest group of people enters the funnel. Then the quantity of people passing through the funnel reduces as the funnel becomes more narrow. Less and less people enter the next deeper level of engagement.

In the church context, this pattern typically divides people into three levels of engagement. First is someone who makes an effort to connect with the church, typically by attending the main worship service. Next is someone who takes a step to grow in a deeper relational way with the church. And third is someone who actively serves in the church. Although many terms could be used to describe the stages in the funnel, this text will use Connect-Grow-Serve. If a fourth stage is added, it is typically placed at the end as "Go" or the similar, but this is not common, at least in function.

Based on hundreds of congregational surveys, Will Mancini concludes that the percentage of people entering each stage remains consistently rigid in churches no matter what effort is given to move people "forward."[14] About half the people in the first stage enter the second, and then half again of those enter the third. So a typical church assimilation funnel looks like this:

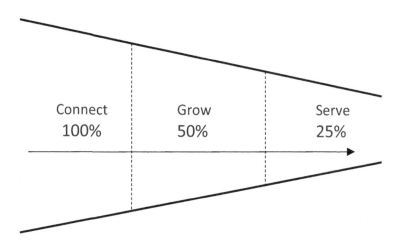

Weaknesses of the Funnel

The assimilation funnel model provides helpful and usually clear next steps for new church attenders and members. It provides an efficient way to organize the ministries and

---

[14] *Future Church*, 215.

programs within the church. Plus, it's easy to measure the level of participation at each stage. Most importantly, it's great at (designed for?) recruiting the myriad of necessary volunteers to operate all those ministries and programs every week. There's just one major problem. It is largely ineffective at measuring if the church is achieving it's given mission of making disciples who can go and make disciples. Why? Because that doesn't seem to be its goal. Therefore, it's not set up to measure that goal. And that's a major concern because Jesus gave us a very easy metric to see if we're fulfilling his commission—are we making disciples?

Perhaps the greatest weakness of the funnel model is that it appears to have a dead end! All roads lead to Serve, and that almost exclusively means to select a ministry area in the church which occurs in the building during a meeting time in which you can volunteer to serve. Now we all should have a heart to graciously serve the people in our church (I'm on three service areas teams in my church). However, it seems like the primary, almost exclusive, purpose of this model is to generate volunteers. The evangelical church in the West has perfected this process. This would never be stated from the pulpit or in any other church setting, but *in practice* these leaders have adopted the commission of "go and make volunteers" as their primary mission.

The Mailroom Mentality

Another weakness of the assimilation funnel is that assimilation literally means to make everything the same. Everyone follows the same path and ends up in the same sphere of serving. This is great for organizing people (which certainly is important), but does it ever become about disciples making disciples? Or is it more of a "mailroom mentality" that keeps track of the volunteer needs of the church and recruits someone to fill the need (the empty slot), placing people into each ministry "slot" where the member seems to fit?

Because most churches are so desperate for volunteers, they run the great risk of stifling the spiritual growth of their most fervent members who are greatly serving in the church. Note this warning from Harrington and Wiens in *Becoming a Disciple Maker*:

> "Young adults" (Stage 3 – Kingdom-focused Christians) are a joy for church leaders. But please note, it's easy for church leaders to rely on such people for *their support of the church and her programs*. We rely on these people and unconsciously keep them in their place of service. They can often get so busy doing things at church that they do not have or make time to develop to the next level and become personal disciple makers. *If they don't grow to the next level after years of serving, they will often become stunted and unfulfilled.*[15]

A Better Way

An opportunistic leader looks to see how they can utilize and expand the giftings of church members rather than simply viewing the members as the workers needed to fill the needs of the church. Although the end may be the same (a person serving in a particular ministry), the direction from which that conclusion was arrived at is very different. It is simple to see a person and think, "What responsibility or need can they fill in our church?" Too easily people are reduced to not much more than human resources needed to fulfill our ministerial goals, albeit even with the best of intentions.

---

[15] *Becoming a Disciple Maker*, Bobby Harrington and Greg Wiens (Franklin, TN: Discipleship.org, 2017), 52.

A better view is to see a church member and consider, "What does God want to do with this person in our church? How does God want them to develop here? How far do we think God wants to take them in leadership?" This is a long-term approach but it is truly the perspective of God that we should pursue.

Most churches are not prepared to think in this manner because they do not have a spiritual and leadership development process for members. It is sufficient to simply plug people into filling the operational needs of the church ministry. This certainly is an important reality (we do need children's workers and ushers for the services) but it is where most churches stop. Basic discipleship is rarely a spoken goal, even though it's the primary mission of every church, and leadership development doesn't even enter the grid.

"Funnel Fusion" – Will Mancini and Cory Hartman

Will Mancini and Cory Hartman thoroughly analyze the assimilation funnel and what they call the multiplication funnel of Jesus. They propose a "fusion" of the two funnels in their book *Future Church*.[16] They describe the assimilation funnel as an inward funnel, representing people entering into deeper levels of engagement in the church organizational structure. The multiplication funnel is an outward funnel, representing the church members' increasing impact outside the church into their community, region, and even the world, following the fashion of Acts 1:8, but with a focus on personal discipleship. Mancini and Hartman propose that the solution for a healthy church is to "fuse," or combine, the two funnels. It appears as below, but with my addition of the fourth stage of "Go" in the multiplication funnel.

---

[16] *Future Church*, see chapters 13-15.

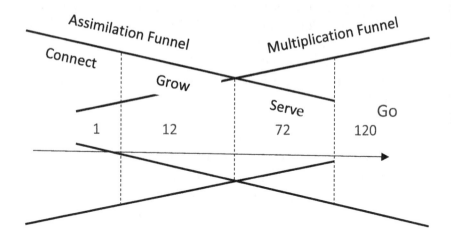

Connect-Grow-Serve-Go sounds like a great process. It even has a "catchy" alliteration and rhythm with Grow and Go (in English)! The challenge, of course, is in the implementation. Reaching the "Go" stage should be the goal of a church committed to making disciples. But a foundational inconsistency will doom the process to failure in reaching "Go" if the church is not aware of it.

Connect With What or Connect With Whom?

As was previously examined, the first stage Connect of the assimilation typically takes place when someone attends a church service (which in today's world could be online). So the visitor Connects with the church. Then we want them to take a step to Grow in the church or a church function. Next, they are to Serve in the church. Do you perceive the trend? Every stage to this point is *with* the church and usually even *in* the church. If that is the case, how do we expect members to reach the fourth stage and suddenly be able to Go *outside* the church and reach someone for Jesus? It's simply not going to happen on a regular basis.

So Go must, once again, be connected with the church. The church must organize an evangelistic activity or event because the members have never been prepared to reach out on their own. Evangelism (the ability to share the Gospel personally with someone not following Jesus) has been almost entirely reduced to "invite someone to church" so the pastor can present the Gospel.

What if we inverted the focus from "bring people to church activities" to "let's equip all our church members to go and make disciples?" That is the mission Jesus gave us, isn't it? The church could train and encourage its members to connect with people in their sphere of relationships and present the Good News of Jesus. Through personal discipleship (not necessarily one-on-one), the church member, who is now a functioning disciple, could help the new believer grow in Christ. Together they can serve in the church *and* their community. And all disciples could be truly prepared to go and make more disciples in any setting.

Inverting the focus of the church does not in any way diminish the importance of corporate church activities. Once again this is not an either/or scenario. As disciples connect with people outside the church, the "outsiders" will naturally integrate into the church body. They will connect with the "what" of the church as they have connected with the "whom" of the disciple. It will be a joy for them to do so, as they come into the fellowship that can only exist among followers of Christ. However, the church activities should be designed to encourage and support the primary mission of the church—go and make disciples!

Cycles Instead of Funnels

Perhaps another weakness of a funnel description of the disciple making process is that it's linear. As a diagram it goes to infinity, I guess, off the right side of the page (or sign)! A better design to represent a process is a cycle.

As an example, let's consider the original assimilation funnel Connect-Grow-Serve as a cycle. We have already discussed that a final stage of Serve seems to have little outflow or growth potential. The question for the church member becomes, "What's my next step?" If it's a cycle, then the process goes back to Connect. This would indicate to the serving church member that he should connect with the new people entering the cycle as they connect with the church. And in essence that does happen as they are serving in church programs and activities. But the full three-step cycle takes place almost exclusively in the church, as represented in the following diagram with the church building as the dominant feature.

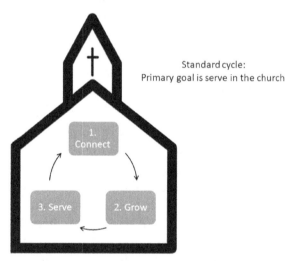

Standard cycle:
Primary goal is serve in the church

A better sequence is to switch Grow and Serve to put Grow as the third step. This means that spiritual growth is the "destination" for the church member. Of course, there is no end to spiritual growth, so this certainly seems like a great aspirational goal for the member. However, this also increases substantially the onus on the church to plan for and provide growth opportunities for the church members. In other words, the church must develop practical ways to continue to *invest* in the long-term spiritual growth of the members, not just *receive* from their service.

In a cycle, Grow would lead back into Connect. The cycle looks like this, but it seems like there's still a missing piece.

Better: Connect - Serve - Grow

As was seen in the "funnel fusion" diagram, the missing piece is Go. Although the Great Commission is not simply "go" but "go and make disciples," I contend that making disciples does not function well without the mentality to first "go"! We cannot separate the go from making disciples.

Even Better: Connect - Serve – Grow - Go

The four-step cycle diagram appears on the following page. Now the cycle makes much more sense. Go leads back into Connect, which is exactly what we want. But in this model the disciples have the focus to go and connect with people ***outside*** the church who are not following Jesus, with the church serving as, in essence, the equipping and sending base. The disciples will serve those people, winning them to Christ, helping them grow through discipleship, then help the new disciple go and do the same cycle with others who need Jesus! This cycle is the "generator" of healthy church multiplication.

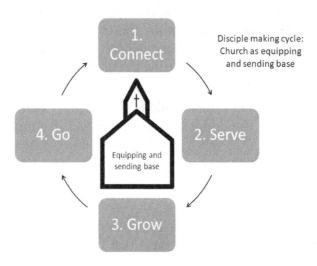

In this model the church is still in the center, but the building is much smaller because it does not dominate and consume the majority of activity of the members. In fact, a major focus of the disciples in the church is now going and making disciples *outside* the church building. The church is a base that prepares and supports its members to fulfill the Great Commission.

The purpose of this chapter has been to help prepare you for the remainder of the book by beginning to think in the form of processes. The process concepts examined are still mostly oriented toward a Western mindset. I'm sure our brothers and sisters in regions of the world where the church is truly exploding could substantially contribute to this analysis! However, no matter the setting and culture or church organizational structure, church leaders are still responsible to facilitate an easy and effective process *to go and make disciples who can go and make disciples.*

Chapter 6

Making Disciples—Mend the Nets!

Before entering the process of designing your equipping track, we need to delve deeper into two stages that are key in any equipping process—making disciples and preparing leaders. The former will be examined in this chapter while the latter is the subject of the next chapter.

Making disciples that can go and make more disciples is the basic fulfillment of the Great Commission. If we are to be obedient to Jesus Christ our King, then this must be the basic requirement of our spiritual and ministerial life. The call and mandate to ALL disciples of Jesus is to go and make disciples. It is not optional for us as Christians. It is also not optional for a church to choose not to embrace this mission at its very core.

It would be good to begin with some basic definitions in relation to making disciples because the word discipleship can mean very different things to different people.

Disciple (a noun) – A person who has surrendered their life to follow Jesus as their Lord and who seeks to emulate Jesus in all their ways (behaviors and thoughts) through the power of the Holy Spirit. Alan Hirsch describes a disciple as someone who is "doing the kind of things that Jesus did for the same reasons that He did them."[17]

Discipleship – The lifelong process of becoming more like Jesus and completing the assignment God has prepared for every disciple of Jesus.

Disciple/Discipling (a verb) – An intentional relationship, founded on God's word, between two or more disciples with the goal of seeing Christ formed in each person, typically with

---

[17] *Becoming a Level Five Multiplying Church Field Guide*, 110.

a more experienced disciple and one or more less experienced disciple(s) or seeking "pre-disciple." (Matthew 28:19 is the verb form – "*disciple* the nations.")

At times the expression a "biblical disciple" has appeared in this text. The purpose is to emphasize what a disciple of Jesus really should be like according the Bible. I do not equate a person who has made a salvation decision as automatically being a disciple, at least not yet. They would typically be classified in this text as a new believer. Nor do I think the oft spoken concept of "we need to be a disciple before we can make a disciple" is quite accurate. Part of *being* a disciple is *making* disciples. Some have proposed that a believer is not fully a disciple until they are obeying Jesus in making disciples.

There is something I think we all can agree on. The opposite of a biblical disciple is a Christian consumer. This is a person who says they have received Jesus and is attending, at least to a degree, church services and activities. In fact, they may be receiving a lot from the church and Christians. But their primary motive seems to be little more than taking advantage of all the truly wonderful ministries the church has. They are "producing" little if anything in the lives of others. The door of the church is always open to such people, but it should never be our goal for this person to stay in this phase. Don't be *content* just to count another participant—be *intent* on making biblical disciples!

Then there is the question of the process of biblical discipleship. What does that include? How long does it last? What is the best setting, a classroom? Doesn't discipleship happen in our small groups? Isn't discipleship risky or even dangerous? What really is discipleship?! Questions do indeed abound but one simple concept brings much clarity.

Foundational versus Formational Discipleship

It is very helpful to divide discipleship into two general stages—foundational and formational. Grant Edwards does a fantastic job using the construction of a house to clearly illustrate the stages.[18]

Foundational discipleship is like the foundation of a house. Every house needs a foundation, it's mostly unseen (underground), and it's basically the same regardless of the type of house built on it. Foundational discipleship has nothing to do with personal giftings and callings. It is typically not of a long duration. Every disciple of Jesus needs this foundational discipleship and it is best in the first 90 days after salvation.

Foundational discipleship is exemplified in the Luke 6 version of the parable of the two builders. Luke 6:48 says the builder "dug down deep and laid the foundation on rock." The storms and floods *will* come. Only the house (disciple) that has a deep foundation on the rock will survive.

Formational discipleship begins after foundational discipleship and is of a longer duration. It's the house on top of the foundation. It may include small groups, specific retreats, or training programs. Formational discipleship takes into consideration the calling of each person and prepares them to fulfill their calling. It will get more specific to their calling as a person grows in their spiritual maturity.

The Right Material and the Right Delivery Method

A vital key in discipleship is understanding the right *material* and the right *delivery method* to be used in each stage of discipleship. Concerning *material*, just like the foundation of a house is basically the same regardless of the type of house

---

[18] *Discipleship That Works*, 34-35.

built on it, the material used in foundational discipleship should stay to the very basics of our Christian faith. Just like a foundation is underground and largely unseen, the material should have a focus on helping the new believer establish a personal and fruitful relationship with Jesus. A duration of 8 to 12 weeks is typical and sufficient for the material of this stage. Basically it should focus on the first 90 days after a salvation decision.

Just like styles of houses can be very different, the materials used in the formational discipleship stage can have a great degree of variation. It will typically begin with general topics that a church may want all members to go through, including specific short-term small groups, a basic membership class, or additional material used in a one-on-one or a micro-group setting. It may be helpful to think of what you want to include in the "next 270 days" after the first 90 days of foundational discipleship to complete a year-long basic discipleship track.

While the equipping materials used in foundational and initial formational discipleship seem fairly straightforward, the greatest errors are made in the *delivery method* of the materials. Churches have a great tendency to centralize activity in the building, especially whatever is perceived to be "training." The default mentality is most often, "Let's put them in a classroom. It's safer that way because we can control the quality." May I suggest that does little to "equip his people for works of ministry," nor is it the best delivery method for discipleship.

Best practice for discipleship—the sooner the activity takes place after a believer's salvation decision, the smaller the setting should be.

Foundational discipleship should take place one-on-one or in a micro-group of no more than four people (a discipler plus up to three, like Jesus and his three). It simply cannot effectively take place in a classroom or even a small group because it must reach a level of relationship that allows and facilitates the freedom and permission to truly get involved in someone's life.

Mend the Nets! Get Everyone Ready to Make Disciples

The ideal is that foundational discipleship takes place within 90 days of a person's salvation decision, but the truth is that our churches are full of people who have never been discipled. As a result, they have little idea of how to make a disciple, which is the calling of God for every disciple. As a test, if you asked 100 church members if they could please disciple Brother Joe who just received Jesus as his Lord last Sunday, how many of the 100 would know what to do or even how to begin? (Would you know what to do?)

A healthy goal for a church is to get *every member* through a foundational discipleship study in the *right delivery method* setting of one-on-one or micro-groups of three or four. The best material is simple and easy for any disciple to lead another person through it. The material will also help each group member to learn how to better share their faith (a severe lack in most churches) and will facilitate the micro-group members to pray for the salvation of friends and family. When the group has completed the material of 8-12 weeks (about 90 days), then each group member can invite one or two new people to join him to form a new micro-group and go through the foundational discipleship material with them. The 90 day cycles can repeat as often as desired and micro-multiplication (from Chapter 3) is now exploding!

Remember the 80% hole in our nets that was discussed in Chapter 3? We are losing at least 80% of new believers within 90 days of their salvation decision. Getting as many people in our churches through a foundational discipleship experience and prepared to lead someone else through one is absolutely the best and surest way to close that nasty hole! We can flip that 80% loss rate to an 80% "keep" rate by implementing widespread foundational discipleship in our churches. But remember—use the right material and the right delivery method. (See the appendix for the right material.)

The Church is Not Meeting the Standard

We must take action because the church is not meeting the standard. If our measure of success in discipleship is that a maturing disciple can personally carry out the Great Commission of going and making another disciple, then how does what our churches are offering stack up to this goal? Are we meeting the standard of achieving the mission Jesus gave to us?

Here is a short list of what churches typically offer in what they might view as discipleship:

- A new believers' class of about 10-12 weeks on biblical foundations (almost exclusively in the church building).
- A basic doctrines class that is often a requirement for church membership or water baptism (almost exclusively in the church building).
- A four-week "growth track" typically after weekend church services (in the building). This is often called a growth track, but it is really an onboarding mechanism to join the church. This is a great idea for membership, but not much of a growth track can be accomplished in four hourly class-setting meetings. And it in no terms could it be considered discipleship.
- Small group leaders' training. This could meet some of the standards of preparing people for discipleship, except that most small group environments do not really facilitate functional discipleship relationships.

Discussion and learning is taking place, but it rarely gets to the personal level of discipleship.
- Short-term classes or seminars. Some topics could definitely help prepare people for discipleship relationships, which is productive. The question is if systemic discipleship ever takes place after the classes or if that is ever the intent.
- Producing quality CDs, DVDs, USBs, and print curriculum of the teachings of the pastors.
- Many churches have bookstores well supplied with quality books and teaching materials.

While these church activities can be productive for specific purposes, it is clear that none of them create both the relationships and environment that allow systemic discipleship to take place.

As a result, *less than 5% of churches in the USA* have a disciple making culture and are mobilizing their members to be personal disciple makers.[19] Unfortunately, the reality is that most church leaders overestimate the effectiveness of their church in discipleship and disciple making. Plus, delivering a quality sermon plays a vital role in the church, but it could never be classified in and of itself as anything more than a small aspect of discipleship. The goal of a sermon should be to support the disciple making process in the church by providing sound doctrine.

Discipleship must begin with church leaders. We are quickly losing a discipleship culture in our churches. We must heed these words of warning by Harrington and Wiens:

> "Somehow in the West, we have adopted a model of ministry that precludes making disciples. I went to

---

[19] "National Study: The State of Disciple Making in US Churches," discipleship.org, 2024.

seminary and found that I wasn't expected to make disciples.[20] Most church staff are not modeling disciple making. Ironically, that's not expected anywhere else in the church either. By eliminating both the call to and practice of making disciples, we have essentially neutered the Church in the West."[21]

Evangelism and Discipleship

Using the standard of making disciples who can go and make more disciples as our goal, every church member should be equipped to effectively share the Gospel message of salvation with someone who is not following Christ. The church is falling woefully short in this measure, and the problem is much more severe than most leaders realize.

To begin, according to a survey in 2020, 41% to 46% of people in the USA who identity with a Pentecostal, Protestant, or evangelical church believe that a person can earn their way to heaven through good works.[22] In other words, they do not even believe the basic truths of the Gospel. Further, a 2022 survey reveals that 66% of American Christians are not familiar with "any methods for telling others about Jesus." Perhaps even worse, 52% of the respondents of this same study believe that encouraging someone to change their religious beliefs is "offensive and disrespectful."[23] In other words, they have accepted the lie that "loving" someone means not offending the person rather than sharing the truth of the Gospel that will save their lives from an eternity in hell

---

[20] *Becoming a Disciple Maker*, 21-22.
[21] *Becoming a Disciple Maker*, 22.
[22] https://www.thegospelcoalition.org/article/survey-a-majority-of-american-christians-dont-believe-the-gospel/, accessed 02/26/2024.
[23] https://www.christianpost.com/news/two-thirds-of-christians-dont-know-methods-for-sharing-jesus.html, accessed 02/26/2024.

(that is, if the "Christian" still believes in hell). We are experiencing a crisis in what could only be described as *disobedience* to Jesus' command to the church. This is clearly a pervasive problem of not teaching sound doctrine based in a biblical worldview in our churches.

If you, as a leader, do not believe this lie and are teaching the true biblical doctrine of salvation, then you *must determine* to equip your people to do the same! You cannot assume in this day that church members understand the biblical Gospel, but you *can* assume that even if they do, most do not know how to effectively share it with another person to the point they could personally lead that person to Christ. *This is the basic mission Jesus gave to every believer until he returns.* How can we be so consumed with everything else in the church when this basic foundation receives so little attention? We need to put first things first.

One major step a church can take to equip their people to share the biblical gospel with the right heart is by implementing a foundational discipleship process church-wide as discussed earlier in this chapter. Quality foundational discipleship material will not only anchor disciples into a clear understanding of the biblical gospel but will also prepare them to more effectively share the good news. Then they will be ready to take new believers immediately through the discipleship material!

Leaders need to understand and teach that discipleship begins before salvation. Ralph Moore, founder of the Hope Chapel movement, frequently says that we should "disciple people to Christ."[24] Just like we invest time in people after their point of salvation in discipleship, we should begin before they receive Christ. Then the new believer has a model to do

---

[24] *Equipping Everyday Missionaries in a Post-Christian Era*, Ralph Moore (Exponential, 2022), 17.

the same thing with another non-believer. And multiplication begins to take place!

This is not simply a "nice" idea, but highlights the critical role that evangelism has in the discipleship process. Truly there is no separation between evangelism and discipleship; they work together in the same process. In fact, discipleship without an evangelistic component is doomed to failure. Without new wood the fire will go out. We are called to GO and make disciples. That means we need to go and find people who need Jesus, and they are all around us. Let us heed these strong but true words, "Discipleship without a healthy element of reaching lost people is not discipleship; it is *training for stunted growth Christianity.*"[25]

A Basic Model of Biblical Discipleship

Basic biblical discipleship is simple; it is not complicated. But we avoid it because it's usually not easy! The best scripture for discipleship is well-known:

> "And the things you have heard me say in the presence of many witnesses entrust to reliable (faithful) people who will also be qualified (able) to teach others."
> 2 Timothy 2:2 NIV (ESV)

That's it. Discipleship is that simple. Paul intentionally invested in Timothy whom he calls to invest in someone who can invest in someone. Please note that Timothy was to invest into a person until that person was *able* to do the same. Biblical discipleship requires true multiplication. Discipleship to at least the fourth generation should be our goal.

But Paul invested in more than Timothy. Throughout the

---

[25] *Becoming a Disciple Maker*, 15.

New Testament, Paul's name is listed with at least forty-seven men and women that benefitted from Paul's investment in their lives.[26] God calls all disciples to do the same. And leaders are responsible to systemically establish this priority in the church.

It is the perception of many people that discipleship must be one-on-one, a mature disciple with a less mature disciple. In fact, the relationship between Paul and Timothy is often cited as the prime example, along with Barnabas and Saul (Paul). Certainly discipleship can be one-on-one, but it is not correct to say that only one-on-one is "true" discipleship.

In fact, my experience has shown the opposite. Aside from the obvious caution of dependency and the high demand of time for everyone to be discipled, the greatest weakness of one-on-one discipleship is that there are only two "levels" of spiritual maturity involved. The result is the "flow" of maturity is mostly in one direction, the mature disciple to the less mature. However, in my perspective (and the Bible seems to back this up), any group of people can be divided into three levels—fathers (mothers), young men (women), and children (1 John 2:12-14). A micro-group of a leader plus two or three other participants allows all levels of maturity to truly participate and invest in one another. It facilitates a powerful dynamic and the group is not dependent on the leader. In fact, the micro-group can still meet and have a very productive time even in the absence of the "leader."

I have never experienced participants in a micro-group willing to be vulnerable only with the leader (the discipler). It's quite the opposite. Once someone shares about a struggle, everyone else starts to share about their own challenges and no one feels alone or isolated in their struggle. We call this the "popcorn" effect. It may take a moment for the first person to

---

[26] *Becoming a Disciple Maker*, 19.

speak up (the first kernel to pop), but after that it may be hard to end the meeting!

In reality, Jesus had his three (Peter, James, and John) who received more of his attention than the other nine apostles. As recorded in scripture, Jesus always took all three of them *together* with him for more intimate instruction. I think this is a good model to follow. We call them 3D groups and we encourage all disciples to seek to disciple three other disciples to the point that all three of them can disciple three more. This may be as simple as leading them through the foundational discipleship material and helping them do the same with others. This multiplication of disciples making disciples will generate incredibly healthy church growth!

A major advantage of discipleship micro-groups is that they can be implemented in any church ministry structure. They can function almost like the unseen "undercurrent" beneath the waves of other church activities and programs. The discipleship micro-groups can fit into any organizational structure, supplying a firm foundation of healthy multiplication and generating a multitude of disciples who are truly capable of reaching new people for Christ and effectively ministering to them. Wouldn't any pastor want a church full of this kind of disciple?

One final point about biblical discipleship. If a longer-term discipleship relationship is the goal (perhaps a year as an example), it certainly can include going through a workbook or curriculum, but it should not be limited only to that. Especially for new believers, it is wise to utilize a foundational discipleship curriculum, typically a workbook that the new believer can keep and refer to as many times as he desires. (The new believer will one day go through this book with another new believer!) Further, the discipleship pair or group can periodically decide to go through a book or teaching series. Of course, they can always select a book of the Bible to study together.

What I strongly suggest is that the discipleship be centered on three questions that are asked every time they get together. These questions will help keep the discipleship focused and spiritually healthy. All participants in the discipleship relationship, even the "leader," should answer these three questions:

1. Revelation – What has God been speaking to you? (through the Bible or prayer)
2. Testimony – What victories or struggles have you had since we last met?
3. Outreach – Who are you praying for to receive Christ? (the discipleship group can work together to reach these people for Jesus)

I want to end this important chapter on biblical discipleship with a vital question that will lead us into the next chapter. We are all crying out to God for revival (or awakening) in our nations. But carefully consider this question:

If we are not truly discipling new believers now, how do we expect to be able to faithfully care for the true awakening in our community or nation when it comes?

Let's determine to obey the commission of Jesus to go and make biblical disciples so that we can be ready to receive the awakening. Amen!

PS – In the appendix you will find information about the discipleship materials available through Missio Global.

Atomic Discipleship

Chapter 7

Sending Capacity

As we have seen, making disciples that can go and make disciples is the basic fulfillment of the Great Commission. It is also *the* foundation of church multiplication. It is true that churches can grow (unfortunately) without intentionally making disciples, *but only by addition*. The church can rely on great church-based programming, fantastic facilities, pulpit-centered teaching, great technology, marketing, campuses, etc., to steadily increase their attendance and tithes. It can be wonderful and enjoyable to participate in churches like this that are growing by addition. And some disciples are probably being made, but not intentionally and systematically. It's a random accomplishment that depends more on the initiative of the individual disciple than the church ministry structure. Most importantly, a church will never enter into multiplication using methods of addition.

The methods for church growth in the previous paragraph are what Wilson and Ferguson describe as common macro-addition activities that churches use to create local capacity for numeric growth, regardless of the activity's connection to biblical discipleship.[27] According to a recent survey, about 23% of the churches in the USA are growing numerically by these addition methods.[28] *Only 27% of churches overall are growing*, so church growth in the United States is almost exclusively attributed to these addition methods.

What is certain about a church that is growing by these common macro-addition methods and not by systematically

---

[27] *Becoming a Level Five Multiplying Church Field Guide*, 56.
[28] "National Study: The State of Disciple Making in US Churches," Discipleship.org, 2024.

making disciples is that it has a limited *sending capacity*. I believe the concept of sending capacity is very useful because it can be used in both a micro and macro evaluation. At the micro level, does the church have a good capacity to make and send a disciple to win his neighbor for Christ? At the macro level, what is the capacity of the church to make a trained leader and send them (with a team) to plant a church in a neighboring city or state? A church's sending capacity is the "go" in go and disciple the nations.

As discussed in Chapter 3, building toward macro-multiplication should be the goal of every church. This occurs when the church is intentional in reproducing and planting new churches. But a healthy macro sending capacity requires internal micro-multiplication of disciples first. That's the basic building block of church growth. Church growth and multiplication begins with the capacity of a church member to personally win a person to Christ and equip that person to do the same with another person.

When micro-multiplication is steadily occurring, the church is ready for the next step of creating the capacity to train and develop emerging leaders who can ultimately be sent. This is where the stage of leadership training enters the process.

Essential Elements of Leadership Training

Leadership training is essential for the church to continue to grow and reproduce. Highly effective leadership training can take place in the local church. In fact, it is almost always the best scenario. Why should the local church provide church-based leadership development? Here are some great reasons:

- *The training can fit into the ministry "rhythm" of the church.* The participants do not need to stop serving in the church in order to participate in the training.
- *The training is accessible and affordable.* The participants do not need to travel and it's not expensive. The church already has facilities and instructors.
- *The local church is the "laboratory"* where the participants put what they have learned into practice!
- *Local-church based training reflects the emphasis and characteristics* of that particular local church, its region, and its leadership. You can reproduce who you are.
- *Local-church based training will train **multiple times more** church members* than the number of members who would seek outside training.
- And most importantly, local church leadership is preparing developing leaders in their church in *the same way that Jesus trained his twelve disciples and as they are mandated by equipping the saints for the works of ministry!*

So the first essential element of leadership training is that the local church leadership embraces their call to do it! Why would a pastor want to send a church member to be trained by someone else? Or, do you really want an online professor training your people? There is nothing wrong with the quality training offered by institutions, but is that really the best way to train your people? Most pastors greatly underestimate the number of church members who want more ministerial training. It is a primary way that the church can invest in its people. Plus, it's an essential step in reproducing the church.

Another essential element of leadership training is to provide a curriculum that is what I describe as balanced and complete. It's balanced in that it does not focus excessively in one area of training. This could be by topic or style of training.

For example, the topics should be well balanced. Our church-based Missio Global Schools of Ministry have three learning domains, what we call Knowing, Doing, and Being. All 36 modules generally fall into one of the three domains. Therefore, the training is well balanced between Bible oriented modules (knowing), ministry skills (doing), and spiritual formation (being). Balance also includes the sources of the training material. It is best to have multiple sources of textbooks and material to provide a well-balanced training.

The curriculum should also be complete. It needs to include a broad enough number of topics to comprise an effective learning experience. And "experience" is a key word. To be considered complete, the training needs to include a significant amount of ministry experiences, some of the experiences conducted in teams. The goal is not to produce seminary graduates; the goal is to produce leaders who are effective *ministers*. (NOTE: See the appendix for more information on how your church can establish and host a Missio Global School of Ministry.)

Planting Churches

Many church leaders believe (or at least act as if) their church is not called to plant new churches but to simply grow and impact their city or area. However, I believe God expects more. Disciples should be reproducing disciples, and churches should be reproducing churches. While no one would disagree that the Great Commission involves making disciple makers, many Christians and leaders are less convinced about the need to multiply churches. Common questions include:

- Why should our focus be on establishing new local churches?
- Isn't it sufficient to simply grow existing churches?

- Aren't there many small congregations and almost empty church buildings around the world? Can't we begin with them before we plant new churches?
- I am too busy leading my own church. How could I even consider planting a new one?

Reasons to plant new churches are numerous but they all come down to one truth—all healthy life doesn't simply grow, it reproduces! Healthy people don't just grow up into adults, they have children! Here's some good reasons to plant a church:

- New churches often speak to the next generation of young people as well as different ethnic or economic groups better than older churches.
- Multiplying a church often "prunes" the sending church in a healthy way (John 15:2). Underutilized church members take on new responsibilities in the new church and grow in the process. Other members of the sending church take over the responsibilities of those who were sent.
- All congregations will eventually die. Multiplying themselves ensures their continued impact and influence.
- Multiplication of churches not only leads to greater evangelistic results, but also may ensure the survival of Christianity in a culture.

And for our statistics geeks (like myself), consider these:

- In 2010, one major US denomination found that 80% of its converts came to faith in Jesus in churches less than

two years old. (Now that is an amazing stat!)[29]
- In a 2015 study, 42% of church members in new churches either did not previously attend church or had not attended in many years. Other studies have this as high as 60-80%! (They reach the unchurched.)[30]
- New churches reach 3-6 times more people than older churches of the same size.[31]
- And here's my favorite, a church under 200 members is *four times* more likely to plant a church than a church with over 1,000 members.[32]

There Are No Legitimate Excuses

The last statistic above is so startling I need to write it again—a church under 200 members is four times more likely to plant a church than a church with over 1,000 members! Church planting is *not just for big churches*. In fact, there appears to be an inverse relationship between the size of a church and its willingness to plant a new church. Why would that be? Could it be because most of the big church's resources are tied up in a building and a myriad of programs it has to run in order to keep the addition continuing?

It is a clear trend that the more economically developed a culture is, the less propensity there is for the churches in that culture to plant new churches. In an extremely poor nation, any shade tree will do to gather people! But in the West, we need

---

[29] https://www.desiringgod.org/messages/i-will-build-my-church--2, accessed 02/20/24.
[30] https://news.lifeway.com/2015/12/08/study-new-churches-draw-those-who-previously-didnt-attend/.
[31] https://redeemercitytocity.com/articles-stories/why-plant-churches. In pdf - "Why Plant Churches?".
[32] https://outreachmagazine.com/features/10782-small-church-by-the-numbers.html, accessed 02/20/24.

at least $250,000 and at least 40-50 people before we're willing to "risk" stepping out to plant a church.

We see once again that the key to execution (implementation) is simplicity. It is much easier to reproduce something that is simple. I understand the response of some leaders saying, "We need to plant a church in a way that is relevant to our culture." As a missionary and missiologist who planted a cross-cultural church (in a second-language) outside the United States, I can say with experience that I understand that principle. However, I have found that as our primary focus remains as being relevant to the Kingdom, then we and our ministries will be relevant to our culture. Isn't the Kingdom of God what people really need?

Micro-multiplication discipleship is not complicated; it is simple. If this is what can drive the growth of a church, it can drive the growth of a new church plant. I encourage you to avoid the "big launch" trap that we have perfected in the West. It is perhaps the greatest barrier to church planting that we face in more developed nations. And it's a barrier that the church itself has created!

How is a church with less than 200 members able to plant a church? It's because that was the intent of the leader before the original church was planted! Church planting is in the DNA of the leader and all the first members of the church come to embrace that vision as their own. If leaders set this as their standard of success, the people will be unleashed to reach the goal. If you can make disciples who can go and make disciples, planting a church is just the next achievable step! As Eric Hoke has said (and I'm sure others), "If you plant a church, you *may (might)* make disciples. If you make disciples, you *will* always plant a church."[33]

We end this chapter with a final thought about church planting. It's not about building our kingdom, but gaining new

---

[33] https://twitter.com/erichoke/status/1624495131922399233.

ground for the Kingdom of God and seeing many lives transformed. Church planting is the greatest method of evangelism and, therefore, the best way to reach more people for Christ. It is the best way to fulfill the Great Commission of going and making disciples. Let's keep our eyes on the harvest and make disciples, not on adding to the number of churches in our denominations or networks. These words by Harrington and Wiens help us maintain this focus:

> "The goal of multiplying churches isn't simply having more institutional churches on the corners of our communities, but rather to have more bodies of Christ that are committed to, and are practicing, disciple making."[34]

---

[34] *Becoming a Disciple Maker*, 30.

Chapter 8

Define, Design, Implement, Refine

We have arrived at the point of putting together the equipping process! I expect that most readers have already been evaluating the process they have in place and adjustments that could be made for improvement. That is natural and fine. I just want to remind you that the goal is to fulfill the mission Jesus gave to us of going and making disciples. It may look a little different in every church, the methods can vary, but the message and mission cannot. There are probably a number of popular activities and programs in a church that do not directly (or even indirectly) support making disciples. If those programs consume so much time and effort of the church members that biblical discipleship is not taking place, those programs may be among branches that need to be pruned for the vine to generate "fruit that remains."

Define – What is the Desired Outcome?

This chapter will follow four basic steps in process development. The first step is to clearly define the desired outcomes. Following the pattern of Chapter 3 (What Are You Aiming For?) and the discussion of goals, it is productive to define desired outcomes at both the micro and macro levels. For example, what is the desired outcome of the church's impact on an individual (the micro level)? Questions to examine include:

- How would you describe an ideal faithful member of the church?

- What would you hope to be the condition and practices of their personal walk with the Lord? Describe the devotional life you would like them to have.
- What would be their characteristics as well as their competencies?
- How would you like them to be serving and fulfilling God's call in their life?
- How would you describe their ability to impact the lives of other people?
- What other questions could you consider on this list?

Certainly at the micro level the desired outcome for church members is that they are experiencing the fullness of a life-giving relationship with Jesus; that they are living a victorious life in regard to health, family, and finances; and that they continually seek to be in God's purposes for their lives, empowered by the Holy Spirit, impacting lives around them. In short, they are like the disciple Ananias as examined in Chapter 2. There is little question about these desirable outcomes.

At the macro level of church-wide activities, desired outcomes can be a bit trickier to define. We may be quick to describe anointed worship services, powerful preachings, a packed church building during the services, high participation in small groups, tremendous kid's programming, and many salvations. These are all good, exciting and make us feel like "God is really moving." But we have to be very careful to consider the role these macro outcomes have on making the kind of disciples that we just described in the micro outcomes. *The micro and macro desired outcomes have to be in alignment.* If not, it will cause confusion and inconsistencies in the church.

To define macro desired outcomes, the church leadership needs to ask questions like:

- What does a church that has true discipleship in its core DNA look like?
- What steps can the church take to ensure that a majority of church members are involved in personal discipleship?
- What programs do we need? How can we make sure that the programs support or complement discipleship and not interfere with it?
- How can we ensure that all of the primary meetings (e.g., worship services, small groups, training programs) all integrate well with the base of discipleship?
- How does our budget support micro-addition and multiplication (disciples making disciples) and macro-multiplication (reproducing the church)?

The truth is that a "packed church, anointed service" macro outcome is *much easier* than fulfilling the mission of truly making disciples. And therein is the trap, sometimes called the "success trap," where everything looks to be going great, but we're failing in the core mission. Be careful to define biblical and aligned desired outcomes at both the micro and macro levels.

From these desired outcomes (indicators), the next step is to establish goals in all four elements of micro-addition, micro-multiplication, macro-addition, and macro-multiplication. It is possible that one strong goal statement in each of the four areas is sufficient. Then finalize some first-draft outcomes (measurable indicators) for each goal. This is a work in process, so anything can be adjusted as you go forward in developing the process.

Design – What Are the Steps?

With the goals and desired outcomes at the micro and macro levels defined, it's time to begin putting together the elements of the development process. Here are a few guiding thoughts.

First, begin with foundational discipleship as examined in Chapter 6. Do not skip this step! Even a majority of faithful members of any church cannot effectively share the salvation message and have never discipled anyone through the foundations of walking with Jesus. Every disciple of Christ is called to do this! Prepare them, but *not* in a classroom. Just give them the tools they need. (More below in Implement.)

Second, simplicity is critical! It has been rightly said that complexity is the enemy of execution.[35] If the process is too complex it simply will be too complicated for the people of the church to implement. Simplicity also facilitates the church's ability to track success indicators, which is an essential component in the development process. In the end, the objective is to be able to represent the entire process in an easy to follow diagram. This visual dimension of the process will be a powerful tool to provide clarity, direction, and motivation to the church members.

Third, the process needs to be easy to reproduce in any setting. The simplicity of the process will facilitate its reproducibility. This guideline also means that the development process cannot be dependent on the presence of a specific church leader(s). The system itself needs to contain the clear and effective tools needed for any faithful disciple to utilize the process. As stated by Harrington and Wiens, "Spiritual 'parents' (disciple makers) need practical models, easy-to-use tools, and reproducible systems."[36]

Fourth, think in terms of events and processes. Some

---

[35] Tony Robbins.
[36] *Becoming a Disciple Maker*, 54.

elements of the overall equipping process will be events or specific points of completing a step (like a retreat). Other elements will take place over the course of several weeks (specific small groups), months or even a few years (leadership training). It is fine to begin by analyzing all the current church activities and see where they fit in a potential development process, but you must be constantly reinforcing that the goal of the process is to support the mission of making disciples who can make disciples. Some of the current church activities and programs may not fit this goal.

Implement - How to Launch

The previous step of designing a church-wide development process will easily take several months. The leadership team will need an initial round of discussions followed by several rounds of discussions with key leaders, such as ministry area leaders. While it is good to have a goal to implement the development process by a certain date, the "process to develop the process" should not be rushed. The good shepherd does not drive the herd faster than it can go, although the shepherd does need to prod the sheep at times! Obviously the church must arrive at the point of implementation. This is why it began the endeavor of creating a development process—the church is serious about improving its capacity of making biblical disciples.

Perhaps the most important guideline about implementation is this—*it is best not to introduce the new development process church-wide all at the same time.* This is because the new development process will likely conflict with some elements of the existing church culture. And as the famous saying goes, culture eats strategy for breakfast.[37] Leadership cannot force a change in the culture. The better way is to show the fruit of the new process in stages, and then people will get onboard to embrace it.

So what is a good implementation strategy? Take the "leaven" approach—a little leaven will eventually permeate a large batch of dough (Matt. 13:33). Start with a pilot group. As an example, the first step for almost every church in launching an equipping process will be to initiate discipleship following a truly biblical pattern. (This is because less than 5% of churches have implemented a biblical pattern of personal discipleship.) Here are some steps to launch foundational discipleship (as discussed in Chapter 6):

- Select about 12 mature disciples in the church who are radically committed to making disciples.
- Conduct a two to three-hour training and vision casting session with the 12 disciples. Review the foundational discipleship material and explain the discipleship initiative the church is undertaking.
- Have each of the 12 go and find one or two more people who want to be involved in discipleship to form 12 discipleship micro-groups (24 to 36 people total).
- Each micro-group should go through the discipleship material (typically 8 to 12 weeks).
- At the completion of this round of discipleship, each micro-group member can go and find one to three more people and form more foundational discipleship micro-groups.

At this point micro-multiplication of disciples has truly begun in the church. This "bottom-up" approach may seem to

---

[37] Peter Drucker, world renowned management expert.

be a slow process at first, but give it time. Soon it will permeate the church just like leaven in dough!

If you follow this pattern of first establishing foundational discipleship, the spiritual maturity of the church will dramatically increase, as well as the number of disciples. This will prepare the church to implement the next stage of the equipping process that you have developed. In each stage begin with a pilot group.

For a denomination or a smaller family of churches, it is common for one or two key churches to be selected as pilot projects to begin new development initiatives. As success in the pilot church is gained through experience, the development process can be expanded in stages to additional churches. This is wise because it is always necessary to refine the process!

Refine

This is why you want to launch a new development process with pilot groups! You can be sure that refinements will be necessary. This is not recommended, but it is even common for churches to launch new initiatives before the initiative is fully designed. (This is called driving the car before we have all the wheels, something we would never do, right?)

While we always want to do our best to design and develop the new process before it is launched, one helpful tip is what I have heard called the Microsoft rule—put the product out there when it's 98% ready and let the users find the bugs. Adjustments can always be made as the pilot group is going through the process.

Having said that, I highly recommend giving the new process *at least a full year* before any significant refinements are made. New systems take time to show positive effects. This is especially true when the issue is discipleship and leadership development. To be sure, the higher the stage in the development process, the longer it takes the positive results to be seen. For the highest level of leadership development, the church needs *at least* three years to see the full impact. The crops need to grow and be cultivated before they should be harvested. *Don't be impatient and miss the harvest.*

Chapter 9

The Entrance and the Exit

As we move into the final steps of developing an effective equipping process, it is important to examine the role that entering and exiting the stages of the process have on its overall success. They can either constrain or support the success of the equipping process.

The Entrance–A Good Onramp

Clarity of *expectations* is the goal of a good onramp. Just like clear signs for entrances onto a highway, the church must provide a clear entrance into the equipping process. New members need to be able to easily see and say, "I need to get on here in order to arrive there." That is why a simple and memorable visual image or diagram of the process is very helpful.

A good onramp shows you where to get on the highway, but it also tells you where you're going. It's important to define the "there," the destination. The goals you have defined previously determine the destination. And the destination is typically (should be) made clear to the congregation in vision and mission statements. Of course, entire books are written on the subject of these statements, so we won't go too deep here. For our purposes, just be clear that the vision and mission statements should concisely summarize the micro and macro goals that you have defined. It's what you want to "see" in the future (vision) and what you're going to do to get there (mission).

Remember, values → goals → measures; your statements should be based on these. When all the factors are integrated, it will form a clear picture of the destination in the minds of the members.

There is always the question of if people coming in from other churches (transfer growth) need to start the process at step one. If the development model is based on biblical discipleship, as it should be, then discipleship is more of a lifestyle for all members rather than "part of the process." A mature Christian arriving from another church will quickly be able "to get up to speed" on using the foundational discipleship materials of the church and be ready to start making disciples. Using our highway analogy, they only need a short onramp. They may be soon ready to enter into the more developed leadership training stages of the equipping process. In other words, these more mature Christians will follow the same path as newer believers, but perhaps at a quicker pace.

However, any experienced church leader knows there is a word of caution to heed concerning people transferring in from another church. First, do not assume they are in a healthy spiritual state. They may be, but just don't assume they are. Make sure they understand the true biblical Gospel and are living with a biblical worldview. Second, their faithfulness and humility will need a time of testing. Never "promote" someone rapidly just because of their ministry skills or natural abilities. They should receive the same expectations as any new member; make them go through the process like everyone else. Encourage them to be an example for others and the Lord will bless them and promote them in his timing.

Stagnant Church Growth

Every fire needs new wood to keep burning. This dynamic is true for churches as well. If a church is not winning new believers it will eventually stagnate and even decline.

Incidentally, this is why church plants are statistically much more effective at winning people for Christ. They understand they have to win people in order to grow! Established churches with buildings and programs are more focused on (satisfied with?) maintaining the spiritual status quo.

I have heard some church leaders say they haven't implemented basic foundational discipleship because the church has stagnated and there aren't really any new believers in the church. I am reminded of the parable of the two farmers praying for rain (no, this parable is not in the Bible). They both prayed for rain, but one of them went out and plowed the fields expecting the rain. To which farmer do you think God sent the rain? Prepare your church members to go and make disciples. Don't just wait for people to show up at the services!

My ardent advice to the pastor of a stagnant church is to start *foundational* discipleship (remember Chapter 6) in micro-groups of three people. (You could call them 3D groups—"D" for discipleship.) Start with your existing church members. Don't wait to start discipleship until *after* you have "some people to disciple." The 3D micro-group approach will prepare your church members to win people for Jesus and begin multiplication.

Edwards astutely makes this connection between evangelism and discipleship:

"A focus on discipleship equips your church members to *do* evangelism and motivates them to reach out with the Gospel because they feel competent to help a new convert get grounded in their faith. Discipleship doesn't bump evangelism out of the picture—it equips believers to do it!"[38]

Please do not start an evangelism class or an evangelistic campaign to generate some new believers to disciple! Teach church members evangelism in the living model of the discipleship micro-groups that will care for the new believers.

---

[38] *Discipleship That Works*, 209-210.

Evangelism is part of making disciples. Good foundational discipleship material will prepare all micro-group participants, even new believers, to effectively share the good news. (*CrossWalk – Expanded Edition* is written exactly for this purpose. See Appendix.) As part of the 3D micro-groups, each member will be answering the question every week, "Who are you praying for to receive Christ?" (See the "three questions" on page 63.) The group members can work together like "net fishing" to reach those people for Jesus. Then the groups are ready to receive them and make the new believers into disciples who can make disciples. This is true church growth by multiplication!

One final truth for all churches is the fact that the best way to master a skill is to teach what you know. Disciples who are discipling others will absolutely have greater spiritual depth and grow faster in their own maturity. The same is true for the new believers. Put disciple making in their spiritual DNA right from the start. After they have completed the foundational material, help them start discipling someone else. Don't wait for the people to come to church or only pray for revival in your city. Pray, start discipleship and go make the revival happen!

The Exit—Clear Next Steps

Just as in a good onramp, *setting expectations* is critical to the function of a good off-ramp. A good off-ramp sets clear next steps for the church members. Before we go further in this discussion, it should be clear that no one is ever to get off the highway and "park the car" of their spiritual journey. In essence, we never fully arrive at the destination until we finish our race on earth or Jesus returns! In this life, the destination is a lifestyle of having a healthy fear of the Lord, loving Jesus, serving others, and fulfilling his call for each one of us. One day we *will* be with him. Amen!

At the base level of micro-addition and multiplication, the *essential* next step is to equip each member to be able to share the Gospel with someone not following Jesus, win that person to Christ, and equip the new believer to do the same with someone else. This is disciples making more disciples. Once the first generation is set in motion, the disciples themselves will drive this multiplication without dependence on a church program. Personal discipleship is without a doubt the best method to achieve this goal. Yes, church members will also serve in the programs and activities of the church, but that must be understood as a *secondary* next step.

Don't be caught in the funnel that ends with Serve in the church programs. That church will never have the capacity to grow beyond addition and very likely won't last beyond a generation or two. I can show you several churches that I personally know that were vibrant 40 even 30 years ago that are now in severe decline, have actually already closed, or had to merge with a newer church. Don't let that happen to your church. Keep the first things first. Make the expectation clear in the equipping process that the mission of the church (and every member) is to go and make disciples who can go and make disciples.

Shifting now to the phase of leadership training (macro-addition and multiplication), every new initiative in a church is exciting and motivating when it begins! The first class (group) of participants in your church-based leadership training will almost always be the largest, in great part because there are the most candidates available in the first round of training. (Please note that if the church is not growing it will also not have new candidates for future leadership training. Make disciples who can make disciples and the church will always have emerging leadership candidates!)

It should be made clear to church members that the church-based leadership training program is the primary source for ministry leaders in the church. The training program will also prepare future church planters. At the same time, many members may feel like they are not leaders and may be hesitant to enter the training. For this reason, it is wise to have a two-tier training program. For example, our Missio Global School of Ministry model is split into a one-year certificate program and a three-year diploma. All faithful church members are encouraged to complete at least the first year. This will equip all disciples to have a deeper walk with Jesus and be more effective to minister to others. After completing the first year certificate, they have the option to continue two more years or not. This two-tier training allows people to take the "exit ramp" from the leadership training program that they feel is appropriate to their calling.

A factor that can restrict or even kill a good leadership training program is not having clear expectations for those who have completed it. On one hand, the church should not "over sell" what they promise to graduates. One church we worked with recruited students to their new training program by stating that every graduate of the program would be recognized as church missionaries. However, it was forced to withdrawal this promise at the end of the first round of training when it became clear that it would not be appropriate to recognize some of the graduates as church missionaries. A simple adjustment of the expectation to be "graduates will be eligible for consideration to be church missionaries" resolved that issue for further classes.

The other end of the spectrum of expectations is also true. If the graduates are not well utilized in the church, it can seriously dampen the motivation for future participants in the training program. Of course, the graduates should not expect guarantees of having leadership in church ministries handed to them. They should also be expected to take initiative. But the church is investing in these current and future leaders for a reason. Make sure they have a good trajectory for ministry as they complete the training program. (We have experienced the results of not taking this initiative.)

Returning to our highway analogy, these emerging and trained leaders actually do not take an exit off the highway. They take a ramp onto the next highway! Help guide them to that next highway. In our Missio Global Schools of Ministry, all third year students meet at least once a quarter with an assigned church leader as a kind of ministry guidance counselor. The church leader will help the student (and the church) plan for their increasing role in the church upon their graduation. For example, it is the goal of our Schools of Ministry that one out of every ten three-year graduates is sent to plant a church. We always challenge the students with, "Who will be the one among the ten?"

That's a good challenge and motivation for both the students and the church! Will the church be ready to send that person? It is clear how having appropriate micro and macro multiplication goals and the development process to support those goals will keep the church growing in a healthy manner, founded on the Great Commission of going and making disciples. Yes Lord, let it be so!

Atomic Discipleship

Lesson 10

Making It Yours

The Gospel will have a culture altering impact if it is lived out by Christ followers and declared with boldness and supernatural power. History has shown this to be true time and again. The completely pagan and sexually immoral cities of the Roman Empire experienced a community-wide "deliverance" when the first century Christians engaged the culture with the Gospel. This final chapter will address culture, both in the church's discipleship and leadership development process and its impact on the culture at large in our communities and nations.

How Did We Get Here?

I want to begin by "zooming out" to the culture at large for us to get a better idea of what doesn't work well in the church. We have seen some very disheartening statistics in the previous chapters which beg the question, "How did we get here?"

As discussed, you will hit the target at which you are aiming. We cannot avoid considering what we have been aiming at and where we seem to be trying to arrive. Here's some descriptions of where we have arrived:

- *Consumer mentality* – The church has largely become a spiritual supermarket made especially to meet the needs and desires of every church attender or visitor. The number of participants is the main measure of success rather than becoming a true disciple of Jesus.

- *A fear of offending* – Perhaps as a result of wanting more participants, the church as slowly moved into placing a high value on not wanting to offend people. We are never to interact in an offensive manner with people, but the Gospel is an offense. We should not try to be "nicer than Jesus" and love people right into hell. Love demands the truth, and the truth demands love.

- *A crisis of biblical worldview* – In the United States as of 2022, only 37% of pastors have what can be defined as a biblical worldview. Even among evangelicals it is only 51%. By contrast, 62% of pastors have a syncretistic worldview, a mixing of worldly philosophies with elements of biblical Christianity.[39] These are the people preaching from the pulpits and training the next generation. We have become a biblically illiterate culture at large, and even in a large portion of our churches. A biblically illiterate culture will not recognize sin.

- *A misunderstanding of the **love of God** and the **fear of the Lord*** – A common manifestation of this syncretism is the false "love only" gospel that permeates many churches. This false gospel teaches that all our sin is acceptable because God loves us, any identification of sin is "hate speech," and our acceptance into heaven is based on the fact that God loves us (which it's not; it's based on our repentance and acceptance of Christ's work on the cross).

These characteristics indicate how the world (compromise, ungodliness and immorality) has influenced the church more than the church has impacted the world with the goodness, holiness and power of God. Adopting worldly characteristics,

---

[39] "American Worldview Inventory 2022, Release #5." Cultural Research Center, Arizona Christian University, 2022.

such as consumerism and inclusiveness, into our ministry methods, and even doctrines, will never bring what people truly need and actually long for—the eternal Kingdom of God in our midst.

The objective of this list of characteristics is not to bash the church. I have the highest regard for the body of Christ and understand that you cannot love the "head" (Jesus) and not love his "body" (the church). I love the church! But here's the bottom line, which is the purpose of this list—*we reproduce who we are*. A church that exhibits the above characteristics will not only be completely ineffective at making the impact in the culture that God desires, it will be at risk of teaching heresy, also known as doctrines of demons (1 Tim. 4:1).

We cannot remain satisfied, for example, with 52% of Christians thinking its disrespectful and offensive to try to change someone's religious beliefs. That person, if not a Christian, is on a path to spend eternity in hell. We need to take the risk of being seen as "offensive" to share God's love. The example of godly, bold love (the true heart of Jesus) must start at the pulpit. But it can't stop there! It must be systemically implemented throughout the entire church. The best way to achieve that is through biblical discipleship.

A Culture of Going and Making Biblical Disciples

Let's zoom in now to examine the mission of the church. For churches to have a true lasting impact (more than a few generations), we must establish a culture of biblical discipleship. As we just discussed, going and making *biblical* disciples starts with accurately following orthodox *biblical doctrine*. That has to be the starting point. Step one is establishing a *biblical culture* with true abandonment. This is totally radical in today's world and we will receive increasing criticism and even punishment for taking a stand on the Word. Let Jesus be our example to follow.

Step two is to place a high value on true biblical discipleship, taking actions to initiate a *discipleship culture*. A value can be defined as *a belief put into practice*. In other words, if you believe something is important but don't do anything about it, it remains just a belief. Basically all church leaders would say they believe discipleship is important. The ones who do something to put it into practice demonstrate that it's a true value for them. Take the necessary steps to systemically implement true, personal, biblical discipleship in your church.

Step three is being sure to include a *culture of going*. Don't leave this step out! It's where multiplication begins. You must set micro and macro goals and measures for "going." Celebrate the actions that are important in achieving the goals of "going." Schedule periodic special worship services to celebrate the discipleship goals that have been met. Be creative and make it fun. The Great Commission is serious work, but there should be joy in the journey. Celebrate what God is doing as disciples go and make more disciples, the church extends its reach, and new churches are planted.

Culture is an issue that entire books are written about. Seek some out and gain from the insights.[40] A good starting place is simply remembering these steps that help create a culture: values → goals → measures → celebrate. Each element must be clearly visible and repeatedly spoken in the church! It's what defines success for the church. Let your discipleship values determine the goals, define the measures, and direct what you celebrate. That's how a culture is cultivated.

It takes a long time to shift the culture of a church. Some would say it's not even possible. (This is another advantage of planting a new church!) The composition and size of the

---

[40] I highly recommend the resources found at discipleship.org.

church certainly make a difference. A church is like a ship—the bigger it is the longer it takes to make a directional change. Of course, the change always starts with the leadership. The leader must be persistent and loving, but stay the course. The leadership team needs to be on board. Some leaders may need to "get on another ship" because they're not committed to the same destination. Simply start with the pilot group. The fruit is what will gain the hearts of the people more than attempts at persuasive speech.

Reflect Your Church's Culture and Identity

Although the mission of the church is basically the same, to go and make disciples, every local church has its own unique characteristics. Each church has its own "personality" because it has a unique leader and community. Make the equipping process reflect that personality. It's good to let the primary message or identity of the local church come through in the equipping process. Also, it is good to include the local characteristics of your community, city, or region. I am sure a church in Texas could have a different "personality" for their equipping track than a church in Massachusetts (two states in very different regions of the USA). Be creative and even fun with the process.

Our communities need a variety of churches to effectively reach them. No one congregation can reach an entire town or city. Our communities and regions need the entire body of Christ being fully engaged in the Great Commission of going and making biblical disciples. Religion has failed us all. It's not impacting our cities and communities and never will. The unsaved need to see a people who truly have a different spirit and who have an answer that can be *demonstrated*. Don't settle for less than the standard God has set and Jesus commanded us to obey.

Receive God's Plan for *Your* Church

It is totally appropriate and advisable to research the discipleship and leadership development process that other local churches have established. Read several books and even make some visits. This is how we learn. However, please do not make the biggest mistake of not receiving God's plan for your church right from the Holy Spirit. Just as each church is unique, God has a unique plan for your church (while remembering that the mission is truly the same for the Church until Jesus returns). Make the effort and take the time to receive God's plan for your church. You will only be able to persevere through the murmuring and complaints if you absolutely know that you have heard from the Lord. Heed the words of Wayne Cordeiro: "It's always easier to imitate than it is to incarnate."[41]

Trust God and Release Your People to Flourish

The leadership of a Great Commission church must have the heart of being a "sender." Being someone who "holds and accumulates" is completely contrary to the heart of God. For God so loved the world that he *gave* what was most precious to him—*a person, his son!* You cannot hold people back and be in the heart of God. You must trust God and not just release people, but intentionally prepare them and send them. That is the heart of God, your mission as a leader, and the only way the Church will reach the world. *Addition is simply no longer acceptable; we must move into multiplication!*

At the micro level in a church, this means church leadership must trust the people that are being discipled and

---

[41] *Doing Church as a Team*, Wayne Cordeiro (Bloomington, MN: Bethany House, 2004), 123.

Making it Yours

equipped to fully function in their giftings. What does this mean in a practical way? Don't centralize everything in the church building. Resist the tendency of putting all the equipping elements in a classroom setting. Release disciples to personally make disciples. Allow small group leaders to teach and minister. Make disciples and leaders, not just facilitators. If someone causes a problem, correct and pastor them. You must be able to trust God with *his people* and release them to do the work of ministry. Don't be the constraint on multiplication.

At the macro level, do not give into a "poverty" mentality, concerned that the sending church doesn't have the resources to send. Don't think your church is not big enough to send. Don't ever speak, "We'll plant a church when we have enough…(fill in the blank)." That is fear speaking. Determine to ask God to give you the plan for multiplication. Do not settle for less. Most of the time what is not lacking is *faith* to obey God; it's the *courage* to take a risk—actually "step out of the boat!"

Multiplication means as a leader you cannot control everything. So don't try to. Be a releaser and a sender. I have seen ministries miss their opportunity to be a truly influential church because the principle leader tried to control their emerging leaders, which is the primary sign of an insecure leader. As Wayne Cordeiro describes, godly leaders should be "dream releasers," to whom he gives this exhortation:

"You cannot control everything; you are not called to try! Will you trust God and let people function in their callings and even lead?"[42]

I end this book where it started with these thoughts from the preface. Our God and his Commission are still Great, and it's for *every* church and *every* disciple of Christ in *every* nation. It's what the world needs in this hour. The needs are

---

[42] *Doing Church as a Team.*

great but the harvest is greater. Addition is long past being sufficient. We need multiplication. *Let's get going!*

Appendix:
Equipping Resources from Missio Global

Missio Global empowers Christ-followers to become world changers by providing effective and accessible ministry resources to disciples and churches worldwide. Our vision is to see *hundreds* of churches around the world training *thousands* of workers to reach and disciple *millions* of people for Jesus! Dozens of churches in numerous nations are using the Missio Global School of Ministry to prepare leaders and plant churches. For more info:

missioglobal.com   team@missioglobal.org

Resources for REACH

Everyone has an opinion about who Jesus was. This discovery guide looks at who Jesus himself said he was by examining his "I Am" sayings from the Gospel of John. It's great for seekers, discipleship groups, or small groups. (7 lessons)

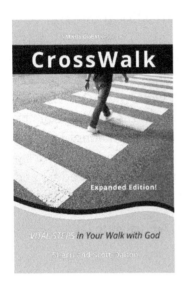

This foundational discipleship study guide is made for all disciples of Jesus. It is designed for one-on-one or discipleship micro-groups. *CrossWalk* is a tool that all disciples can use to make more disciples! It is a key to unlock multiplication of disciples in any church. (the "green" book, 8 lessons)

Resources for DISCIPLE

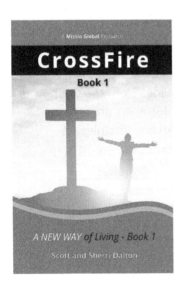

Continuing from *CrossWalk*, *CrossFire – Book 1* delves into biblical values that disciples of Christ need to embrace in their lives. The book is designed for one-on-one or discipleship micro-groups, but is also great for small groups.
(the "red" book, 6 lessons)

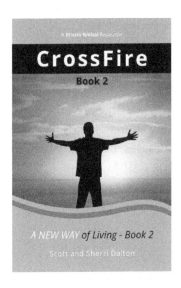

Continuing from *CrossFire – Book 1*, *CrossFire – Book 2* delves into biblical values that disciples of Christ need to embrace in their lives. The book is designed for discipleship relationships and micro-groups, but is also great for small groups. (the "orange" book, 6 lessons)

Resources for TRAIN

Leadership Training

The *Missio Global School of Ministry* (MGSOM) is a partnership between Missio Global and churches around the world. The MGSOM is a valuable and effective training program that is based in local churches around the world. The classes are taught by the local leaders and the program is administered at the local level. It is a proven tool that churches can use to equip their congregation and develop emerging leaders.

Your church can host a Missio Global School of Ministry! Please see all the exciting details about the Missio Global School of Ministry at our website and reach out to us for more information:

    missioglobal.com   team@missioglobal.org

Resources for SEND

Church Planting

Graduates of a Missio Global School of Ministry are eligible to receive "seed" funds to help plant a new church. Funds may not be available for all church-planting graduates, but graduates can apply in coordination with their sending pastor.

Books

Atomic Discipleship: Prepare Your Church to Transform Neighborhoods and Nations

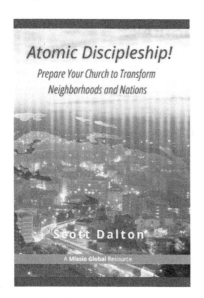

This books serves as a manual for developing an equipping pathway in a local church for biblical discipleship and leadership training. Church leaders are called to equip their people for the work of ministry. The local church is the most effective place to prepare disciples to fulfill their call to transform neighborhoods and even nations! (102 pages)

Bibliography

Barna.com. https://www.barna.com/research/half-churchgoers-not-heard-great-commission/. Accessed 02/02/2024.

Cannon Green, Lisa. https://news.lifeway.com/2015/12/08/study-new-churches-draw-those-who-previously-didnt-attend/. Accessed 02/24/2024.

Cordeiro, Wayne. *Doing Church as a Team*, Wayne Cordeiro. Bethany House, 2004.

Cultural Research Center, Arizona Christian University. "American Worldview Inventory 2022 - Release #5."

Dalton, Scott and Sherri. *CrossFire – Book 1*. Hikanos Press, 2022.

Discipleship.org. "National Study: The State of Disciple Making in US Churches (2024)."

Edwards, Grant. *Discipleship That Works*. Grant Edwards. Specificity Publications, 2024.

Hanewinckel, Jessica. https://outreachmagazine.com/features/10782- small-church-by-the-numbers.html. Accessed 02/20/2024.

Harrington, Bobby and Wiens, Greg. *Becoming a Disciple Maker*. Discipleship.org, 2017.

Hoke, Eric. https://twitter.com/erichoke.

Keller, Tim. https://redeemercitytocity.com/articles-stories/why-plant-churches. In pdf - "Why Plant Churches?"

Mancini, Will and Hartman, Cory. *Future Church*. Baker Books, 2020.

Missio Global. "Missio Global School of Ministry, module 2A – Discipleship & Mentoring."

Piper, John. https://www.desiringgod.org/messages/i-will-build-my-church--2. Accessed 02/20/2024.

Rainer, Thom S. and Geiger, Eric. *Simple Church*. B&H Publishing, 2006.

Strong, James. *The New Strong's Expanded Exhaustive Concordance of the Bible*. Red letter ed. Thomas Nelson, 2010.

Swiger, Mark. *What is a Disciple and How Do You Make One?*. Creation House, 2015.

Warren, Rick. *The Purpose Driven Church*. Zondervan, 1995.

Wilson, Todd; Ferguson, Dave; Hirsch, Alan. *Becoming a Level Five Multiplying Church Field Guide*. Exponential.org, 2015.

Made in the USA
Middletown, DE
25 April 2025

74733358R00060